cooking
for beginners

Written by Emma Crowhurst

Published by Top That! Publishing plc
Tide Mill Way, Woodbridge, Suffolk, IP12 1AP, UK
www.topthatpublishing.com
Copyright © 2013 Top That! Publishing plc
All rights reserved
2 4 6 8 9 7 5 3 1
Printed and bound in China

Contents

... into the fire

Does the world really need another cookbook? There are so many already, on so many subjects. Hundreds of mouth-watering recipes, masses of information, all to inspire and encourage the cook. However, if you've never set foot in a kitchen except to place your cup on the draining board or to get another drink from the fridge, then these books, packed with techniques and ingredients, may as well be in a foreign language.

The excitement and satisfaction of eating something delicious and home-made for the first time when you've never cooked before is unsurpassed and impossible for the experienced cook to envisage.

This flipover will not only introduce you to the pleasure of cooking, but also provide a fundamental and basic view into the kitchen, its necessary equipment, choosing and buying ingredients and an essential collection of easy-to-follow recipes, which will carry you through to becoming a competent, amateur cook. Very few people are born with the ability to be organised enough to cook, but it can be learnt. With some expert tips and advice, you can gain confidence and experience the pleasure of eating non-processed, healthy and delicious food.

Can't cook or won't cook, this book will gently guide you through the ins and outs of cooking, using simple step-by-step instructions and photographs. Get ready to take your first step into the relaxing and enjoyable world of cooking!

Kitchen Essentials

Most labour-saving devices are unnecessary for the very basic cook. Whether you are cooking in a caravan or a castle, the requirements are pretty much the same.

You can use this chapter to help you begin kitting out your kitchen or simply to add a few essentials.

Knives

The most basic item of equipment has to be knives. Kitchen knives must be a good weight, so don't go for the cheapest plastic handles, you need to be able to sharpen them. The top three are:

- A medium-sized cook's knife, with a slightly curved blade for chopping vegetables
- A small knife, sometimes called an office or paring knife
- A serrated or bread knife

An additional knife that can be useful is the palette knife, for turning food in a hot pan.

Paring knife

Bread knife

Palette knife

Knife-sharpening steel

A cook's knife

Kitchen Essentials

Knife sharpening

There are many ways to sharpen knives, including electrical gadgets but many prefer to use a steel, which is a standard chef's tool for sharpening. To use a steel, stand the point on a chopping board, the tip in a cloth to keep it in place. Draw the knife down the steel from handle to tip at a 45° angle. Do this on both sides of the blade evenly and test the knife carefully with your thumb, repeating the process until the blade is sharp. Always wipe the knife after sharpening to remove any metal filings.

Do take care with sharpening – if you get it wrong you may blunt the knives. However, if in any doubt, you can take them to a shoe repair shop – they will usually sharpen knives for a small fee per knife. Finally, do not try to sharpen serrated knives as this will ruin them.

Chopping boards

You need to have at least two chopping boards. They should be made of wood or plastic and be thick and totally flat. They should not wobble when you are chopping and it helps to place a clean, damp cloth underneath to stop it moving while you are cutting.

To clean your chopping board, rinse it first under cold water to wash away meat or food juices and to prevent them 'cooking' into the board. Then, scrub with hot soapy water and a stiff washing up brush, rinse with clean water and dry well. Stand it on its end and allow ventilation space. It is often easiest – and safest – to have one board for raw meat and fish and one for cooked food; catch up on this in the health and safety chapter later (see p. 31).

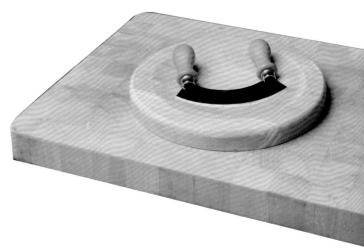

Chopping boards

Kitchen Essentials

Bowls

Metal, glass and plastic are useful, so, if possible have some of each. Glass and metal are easy to wash. If you go for plastic, make sure you wash the bowl really well as plastic can easily be tainted by strong tastes and colours, for example, beef chilli. Metal bowls are not recommended for acidic sauces containing lime or lemon juice (they can add a metallic aftertaste), so use glass for those recipes. Similarly, metal spoons should be avoided for the same foodstuffs, opt for wooden ones instead. The last consideration is that glass and plastic can be microwaved. Skim over any recipe first to check how the bowl and its contents are to be used.

Pots and pans

Glass and metal bowls

Pots & pans

Metal, heavy-based pans are superb for most types of hob cooking and if you get ones that can also go in the oven you save on cupboard space. One or two non-stick saucepans; a griddle pan (pictured middle right) and a medium-sized, non-stick frying pan should cover you for most things. As you expand your collection, copper pots are a useful addition as, unlike conventional pans, they distribute the heat evenly — particularly important when making a delicate sauce that might catch (burn) easily. With all pans, remember to use an oven mitt or pot holder if the handle isn't insulated.

Kitchen Essentials

Wok

If you're a fan of stir fries then you'll find a wok indispensable. With either a slightly flat, or rounded bottom (for use over gas burners), all woks are circular with high sides for fast, high-heat cooking. Choose between a non-stick or carbon steel model but bear in mind that the constant stirring and scraping can remove the teflon coating on non-stick woks.

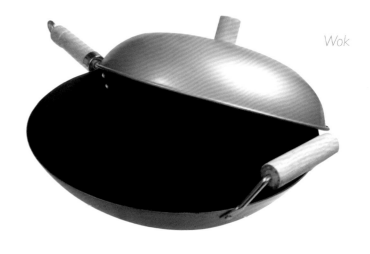

Wok

Baking & cake tins

Roasting and baking both sweet and savoury items requires a few essential items. Make sure you have a non-stick baking sheet, a roasting / baking tin with approximately one inch-high sides and also a cake tin or sandwich cake tins. There are several styles of deep tin to choose from, but one with a detachable base with a clip on the side of the tin makes removing cakes easier.

Pastry cutters

Pastry and cookie cutters are also useful items to have. As well as using them for cutting pastry or biscuits, they are often used when cooking patties, such as the burgers (p. 36) and for shaping desserts such as cheesecakes (p. 88).

Baking & cake tins

Pastry cutters

Kitchen Essentials

A vegetable peeler

A sharp paring knife can be used to peel fruit and vegetables but a peeler is much easier to handle.

Whisks

Balloon (left) or coiled whisks (right) are used for mixing batters, sauces and cake mixes and for beating eggs. Electric whisks can be used for more time consuming jobs, such as whisking egg whites for meringues (see p. 85).

Kitchen scissors

Buy them from a cook shop and keep them just for cooking. Good for cutting up sausages, trimming chicken and snipping bacon and herbs.

Fish slice

A slim one is best but a palette knife will do the same job, which is basically turning delicate food over while frying or grilling. Fish slices also come in handy for stir fries or stirring thick sauces.

Piping bag

A piping bag, and various nozzles, isn't an essential item in your kitchen, but one has been used to add mashed potato to the fish pie on p. 63. They can also be used to pipe cream or icing. Your early attempts may look a bit messy, but just try to apply constant pressure and remember, practice makes perfect.

A vegetable peeler

Wire whisks

Kitchen scissors

Fish slice

Piping bag

Kitchen Essentials

Kitchen tongs

*Perforated /
slotted spoon*

Wooden spoons

Ladle

*Metal colander
& sieve*

Kitchen tongs
Tongs are perfect for grabbing and turning food over, such as sausages, and serving up.

Perforated / slotted spoon
For draining vegetables, general stirring and serving up. Just watch out for hot water and juices dripping through.

Wooden spoons
You want to have a selection of these in different sizes and include a straight-edged spatula in your collection. They are good for all stirring, especially in non-stick pans.

Ladle
This is basically a small bowl with a handle for serving soup, stews and sauces.

Sieves & colanders
These are good for straining cooked vegetables, rice and pasta and, of course, sieving flours. Make sure your sieve is completely dry before sifting flour. Large portions of vegetables, rice or pasta can be easily drained with a colander. Essentially the same as a sieve, although bigger, colanders generally have two handles and often have a base so it can stand in the sink as you use it.

Kitchen Essentials

Measuring equipment

A measuring jug is essential; choose glass or plastic, whichever you prefer. You will also need scales. Electric ones are great, as ounces and grams can be measured accurately, however, basic scales will suffice. Measuring spoons are also really useful for tablespoon and teaspoon measures.

Zester, box grater & hand-held grater.

Measuring equipment

A box grater & hand-held grater

A box grater is perfect for cheese and vegetables. It has four sides, hence the name, and each side has different sized grating holes. Hand-held utensils are more convenient for grating small amounts, for example, nutmeg or Parmesan cheese.

Zester

Great for removing the zest of citrus fruit in delicate strands and a lot kinder on your knuckles as well, but not essential.

Serving plates

Large white plates are excellent for all types of food. Go for all of the same style in large and medium. Big plates make the food look so much better and the space on the plate helps to show the food off (see the section on presentation, pages 33–34).

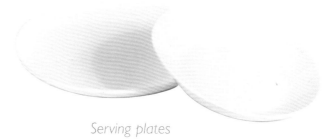

Serving plates

Vegetables

It is recommended that at least five portions of fruit and vegetables are consumed a day. Vegetables, such as potatoes, sweet potatoes, parsnips, swedes and turnips contain starch and sugar for energy. Green vegetables, such as spinach and broccoli are a good source of vitamins and minerals. However, these vitamins are water-soluble so careful cooking and preparation are vital to preserve their goodness.

When choosing vegetables, look for unblemished leaves or skin, and root vegetables, such as carrots and potatoes, should be firm to the touch. As far as portions go, weigh your vegetables before cooking; the combined weight of all the vegetables that you are preparing should be 100 g (4 oz) per person. Once you become more familiar and confident you will find that you no longer need to weigh them, but can rely on your own judgement.

Buying organic
The most important issue with cooking should be the taste. That is, after all, the point. Food produced naturally and in season will always have a better flavour and more nutrients than crops that have been sprayed and cultivated out of season.

Storage
Fruit and vegetables kept in plastic bags or covered in cling film in the supermarket will become damp and slimy if left in their packaging. So, remove any packaging when you unpack your shopping, and store in a cool ventilated place. A vegetable rack in a very cool place is ideal although you can also use the bottom of the fridge. Just make sure you rotate your shopping and don't just place the new veg on top of the old. Salad items should be stored in the fridge and used within a few days.

Preparation
All vegetables should be washed before use, even if they are to be peeled. Only fruit and vegetables that discolour (such as apples and potatoes) need to go into water before cooking. However, if you intend to roast or caramelise them then any browning won't matter.

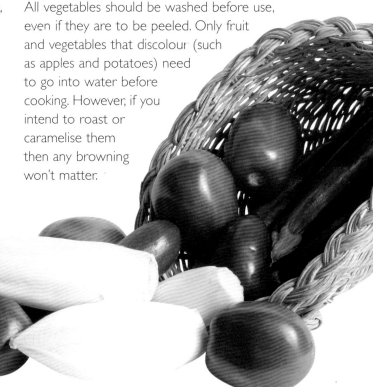

Cooking Methods for Vegetables

There are a number of ways to cook vegetables, from roasting to stir-frying, to steaming and boiling. Modern tastes are not to overcook vegetables and serve them (unless a starchy root vegetable) with some crunch, otherwise known as *al denté*. Should you prefer your vegetables softer than this then cook them for a bit longer, but check them regularly.

General vegetable cooking

Potatoes go into cold, salted water. Bring them up to the boil and simmer with a lid until tender – this usually takes about 30 minutes from cold, then test with a cutlery knife – it should penetrate easily. New potatoes go into salted boiling water and don't need so long.

Batons or rounds of carrot can go into boiling, salted water or be steamed. Cook with a lid for 3–5 minutes, or longer if you like them soft.

Broccoli cooks in the same way as carrots but for about 2 minutes. Leeks take a little longer and should not be served too crunchy.

Exact cooking times are difficult to predict, as it depends on how thick or small the vegetables are cut. The best way to become familiar with cooking times is to test the veg after 2 minutes and then each minute thereafter.

Boiling

Boiling involves placing vegetables into just enough boiling, salted water to cover the vegetables, or placing them in cold water and bringing to the boil. Covering with a lid speeds up the cooking time and saves energy by not losing heat. Boil each type of vegetable separately. Green vegetables and carrots are usually served al denté. Root vegetables are usually served tender, so they can be mashed. In general, root vegetables go into cold water, and are brought up to the boil and then simmered until cooked. Green vegetables generally go into boiling water. However, this is not always so and smaller cuts of root vegetables – such as carrots and new potatoes – should be placed in boiling water.

Cooking Methods for Vegetables

Steaming

Steaming is done by putting a pan of boiling water beneath another pan with holes (similar to a metal colander) to let the steam through. It should be an exact fit and should have a tight fitting lid. Most steamers are sold with one or two layers. Steaming is the healthiest way to cook vegetables, as fewer vitamins and minerals are lost to the water. All vegetables are cooked for the minimum time to reduce the loss of nutrients. If you have the space and do a lot of steaming, then an electric steamer (below) is a good investment.

Bamboo steamers (above) are a good option if you can find one to exactly fit one of your pans. They often have three layers and so save on hob space. You can also buy microwave steamers, and although the vitamins and nutrients may be lost in the microwave, if you suddenly find yourself caught short and needing veg in a hurry, it is always an option. As a general rule, place your veg in a non metallic bowl or microwave steamer with a couple of tablespoons of water, and microwave on full power for a few minutes at a time (or follow the manufacturer's instructions), checking to see whether the vegetables are done. Always allow to stand for a minute, as cooking continues after the microwave has stopped.

Cooking Methods for Vegetables

Stir-frying

Stir-frying is a quick cooking method, which suits vegetables that can be served with crunch, such as carrots, sweet peppers, mushrooms, bean sprouts, baby corn, French beans, mangetout, spring onions and celery. Cut the larger vegetables as thinly as you can and heat a small amount of oil in a wok or large pan. Wait until the oil is very hot and start by adding some crushed garlic and maybe some grated ginger. Then, add the vegetables, starting with the firmest first. Keep them moving in the pan ('stir' frying) and cook until all are just beginning to soften, but still have some bite. Add the bean sprouts last, and finish with soy sauce and a little sesame oil.

Roasting

Roasted vegetables are normally just reserved for Sunday lunch and few people look beyond the potato, or maybe the odd parsnip. In fact, there are a number of vegetables that can be roasted which, when cooked in this way produce the most intense flavours. The real value to roasting as a cooking method is the ease and simplicity of it – while they cook you're free to take on other kitchen tasks. It could hardly be easier to chop a few vegetables and place them in a roasting tray with olive oil and seasoning, then just place them in the oven.

Blanching

Blanching means to slightly undercook the vegetables and then plunge them into very cold water, changing the water a few times so the vegetables cool in the fastest possible time. Then, drain and dry well. The vegetables can then be stored in the fridge until later, then re-heated in the microwave until piping hot or plunged back into boiling water at the last minute. You will lose some of the vegetables' vitamins by cooking them this way, but if you are stuck for time and space this method will take off some of the pressure.

Meat

When choosing meat the recipe will usually specify exactly what sort of cut or type of meat to buy. It can be daunting to go to a meat counter and have to ask for something, especially when you haven't a clue what it should look like. Use a good butcher; they can tell you all about different cuts of meat and what they should be used for – remember it's part of their job to offer advice and assistance.

Tough & tender

There are several factors that affect the tenderness of a piece of meat. The age of the animal must be taken into account. The younger the animal the less exercise it will have taken and therefore the more tender its meat will be. However, some meats, beef in particular, are often 'aged' to improve the tenderness and flavour. The meat is either hung to dry or left in a vacuum sealed bag to retain its moisture.

The other main factor is where on the animal the meat is taken from. The parts of the body that do the most work, such as the legs, neck and shoulders, will be tougher and have more connective tissue. In culinary terms, the more connective tissue a piece of meat has, the longer and slower the cooking time required. These tougher cuts of meat can be cooked in ways to soften the connective tissue, so that it is not obvious when you eat the meat. When connective tissue breaks down it releases gelatin, which gives soft, sticky tenderness. Long, slow, gentle cooking will break down the connective

tissue, leaving a butter-soft consistency to the meat. It is this softening that gives a casserole its richness. It is generally considered that tougher cuts of meat have more flavour.

A common mistake people make is to think that a casserole would be even better with an expensive cut of meat. As these pricier cuts have far less connective tissue, the slow cooking process means that they simply dry out and are fibrous.

Perfect methods of cooking for usually tough cuts of meat are braising, casseroling, pot roasting and stewing. All are moist methods that involve browning the meat and then adding flavoured liquid, such as stock, wine or beer and then cooking slowly in a heavy pan on the hob, slow cooker or in the oven. For tender cuts of meat, the cooking methods are quicker and usually dry. Grilling, griddling and frying are typical ways to cook tender cuts of meat. Roasting is also used for larger tender cuts.

Cooking Methods for Meat

The following terms are often found in cookery books and can be confusing.

Stewing
To cook very slowly in a covered pan with liquid in the oven or on the hob.

Braising
To stew with vegetables in a covered pan in the oven.

Casseroling
Same as the above but in a casserole dish with a lid in the oven or on the hob.

Roasting
To cook in the oven uncovered, usually without liquid, but with some basting.

Pot roasted
To cook in a pot to encourage a moist environment in the oven or on the hob.

Slow cooking
A slow cooker cooks the ingredients very slowly with liquid at a relatively low temperature and for many hours.

Frying
A fierce, stove-top heat cooked with oil or fat.

Grilling
Cooked under a preheated grill.

Griddling
Using a ribbed pan over a fierce, stove-top heat. (Benefits are being able to use less oil and having a ribbed pattern on the meat.)

Beef

There are around 60 cuts of beef, many with different names – so don't worry if you get confused.
Tender cuts of beef are rib, sirloin, fillet and rump (slightly tougher but still considered to be a tender cut). Tough cuts are the shoulders, legs and neck.
Here is a simple run down of methods of cooking and suitable cuts of meat.

- **Braising, stewing and casseroling** – Shin, chuck steak, brisket, flank and neck. Meat labelled for these methods (e.g. 'stewing steak') often will not specify exactly which tougher cut it is.
- **Roasting** – Fore rib, sirloin, fillet (butchers also recommend topside).
- **Frying, grilling and griddling** – Rump steak, sirloin steak, fillet steak, rib-eye and t-bone steak.
- **Pot roasting** – Topside, silverside.

Steak

Learning how to cook steak is a trial and error process. Begin with a nice thick sirloin steak and cut it as you cook it to see what is happening inside. Heat half a tablespoon of oil in a heavy pan or griddle, allow it to smoke slightly, and place the steak, seasoned with salt and pepper onto the hot surface. Cook for 2 minutes each side and then cut a slice off to see what the inside is like. Return it to the pan and continue cooking for another 2 minutes, etc. Another trick to gauge how your steak is cooking is to compare the feel of the meat to the fleshly pad beneath your thumb as you bring your thumb and index finger together, then your thumb and middle finger and so on. You should notice that the pad feels really squishy at first then becomes firmer as you bring the other fingers together; your thumb and index finger feels similar to a rare steak and so on. Quick cooked steaks are better served rare or medium rare. Once the fibres are completely cooked, all moisture is gone from the meat and with the moisture goes the tenderness.

Rare
Hot and bloody but no fibres showing in the middle

Medium
Very hot and pink, some cooked fibres

Well done
Extremely hot and almost no pink, fibres completely cooked

Lamb, Chicken and Pork

Lamb

The same tough and tender rules apply to lamb as to beef. Animals which weigh more than 36 kg (80 lb) are considered to be mutton, and are generally older sheep. However, mutton is increasingly difficult to find these days – which is a shame as it is very tasty. Less than 36 kg and the meat is considered lamb, however, there is a difference between new season lamb and older, larger lambs that are killed later in the year. The younger the lamb, the sweeter and more tender the flesh. Almost all cuts are suitable for grilling, frying and roasting. The fattier, cheaper cuts are better for casseroles. Lamb should be brownish pink when cooked.

Roasting – Leg, shoulder, saddle, best end of neck, loin or breast.
Braising – Chump chops, shoulder or leg.
Grilling, griddling and frying – Best end cutlets, loin chops, and fillet steaks.
Casseroles and stewing – Knuckle, shanks scrag and middle neck.

Chicken

Taste tests have been done with free-range and battery-farmed chickens and the free-range is always the winner. Chicken should always be tender and, as long as you do not overcook it, it will be delicious. One large chicken should serve four people.

Cutting your chicken

When cutting a raw chicken for a casserole, remove the breasts and cut each into two. Remove the legs and divide the thigh and drumstick. You can buy them already cut, but usually drumsticks, thighs and breasts are sold separately. Breasts are perfect for barbecues, roasting, grilling and frying, but always check that they are cooked through (very hot and firm to the touch with no pink flesh). If you are including breasts in a casserole, avoid overcooking them and add them later on in the cooking time. They will not be as succulent or as tender in a casserole. The legs and thighs are more forgiving and are perfect for casseroles and braised dishes.

Pork

The raw flesh should be pale pink and not red or bloody. Pork is generally killed young for the fresh meat market and so is quite tender. The fat and skin are usually removed before cooking, except when roasting, when they make good crackling.

Crackling

To make great crackling you must score the skin with a very sharp knife, through the fat but not to the flesh. Brush with oil and rub on plenty of salt. Roast at a high temperature (220°C / 425°F / gas mark 7) for at least 30 minutes with the fat side uppermost. Once the crackling has formed, turn the oven down to 190°C / 375°F / gas mark 5 for the rest of the cooking time (see table on p. 19).

Roasting Meat

To calculate cooking times of any meat you need to weigh it and then you can use this table to calculate how it should be cooked. All meats need a good 20 minutes start before you apply the formula (see below). Always preheat the oven and cook for the required time – don't be tempted to turn the oven up and reduce the cooking time, you'll simply have a burnt outside and raw inner meat. To test the meat, you can insert a metal skewer into the thickest part and leave for 15 seconds. Then, remove and briefly test on the back of your hand – if the skewer is very hot the meat is cooked, alternatively use a thermometer and refer to the figures below. When cooking chicken, the juices will run clear once the bird is cooked.

MEAT	TEMPERATURE			COOKING TIME		TEMPERATURE ON THERMOMETER
	°C	°F	gas mark	per kg	per lb	
Beef						
To start	220	425	7	20 mins		
Rare roast	160	320	3	35 mins	15 mins	60°C / 140°F
Medium roast	160	320	3	45 mins	20 mins	70°C / 158°F
Well done	160	320	3	55 mins	25 mins	80°C / 176°F
Pork						
To start	220	425	7	30 mins		
Down to	200	400	6	65 mins	25 mins	80°C / 176°F
Lamb						
To start	200	400	6	20 mins +		
Down to	190	375	5	55 mins	20 mins	70°C / 158°F
Chicken Note: *However small the chicken, it will usually take at least an hour to cook*						
To start	200	400	6	20 mins		
Roast	200	400	6	35-40 mins	15-20 mins	80°C / 176°F

Fish

Knowing how to prepare and cook fish, and which fish to use for which recipe is a tricky business. The feel of the cold, wet fish can be off-putting to some, but the flavour and texture of well-cooked seafood is a delight.

Luckily, the preparation of fish can be taken care of by your fishmonger, but it is good to know exactly how it should be prepared for certain recipes; for example, you don't want a trout filleted if you are cooking it whole on the barbecue.

To choose your fish you first need to know if it is fresh. Look for:
• Bright eyes that are not sunken and cloudy
• Firm flesh
• A fresh seaside smell; if your fish pongs it is not fresh
• Scales should not be falling off
• Not too much flexibility

The fishmonger can gut, remove fins, gills and scales, fillet and skin the fish, all to suit your requirements. Some fish will need pin boning (the very tiny bones in trout and other round fish) – this the fishmonger won't do, so a small pair of pliers or tweezers are a great help.

Fish is a valuable source of protein, vitamin D (in oily fish) and most contain little fat. They are categorised in several ways; white or oily; or round or flat.

Oily fish have the oil dispersed throughout the flesh, whereas white fish have the oil concentrated in their liver. Flat fish have four fillets and do not have large scales – examples are: sole, brill, turbot, plaice and halibut. Round fish have two fillets and larger fish have big scales – examples are: salmon, trout, cod, whiting, sardines, mackerel and red snapper.

If you are going to prepare your own fish, you need a fish knife. This is a very sharp, flexible knife that is perfect for taking the fish off the bones and skinning. Use the back of the knife for removing the scales, and scissors for removing fins and gills.

Fish

Cuts of fish

Fillet

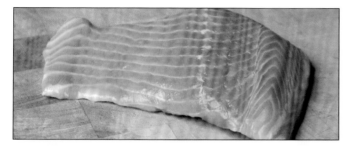

A loin

A steak on the bone

Fish substitutions

Fish and seafood are regional, seasonal and some are overfished, so the type specified in a recipe may not always be available. Here, fish and seafood are grouped with their most suitable substitutes:

- Sole, brill, flounder
- Brill, turbot, John Dory
- Cod, haddock, halibut, hake, monkfish, coley
- Red snapper, red mullet, grouper
- Tuna, swordfish, shark
- Mackerel, herring, sardines
- Seabass, salmon (especially steaks and fillets)
- Mussels, clams
- King prawn, monkfish

Shellfish

Shellfish

There are two main types of shellfish – the crustaceans: lobsters, crabs, prawns, shrimps; and molluscs: single-shell creatures such as whelks and winkles, two-shell or bi-valve creatures, such as clams, oysters, mussels and scallops, and creatures with a kind of internal shell, such as squid and octopus.

Lobsters and crabs can be placed into hot water and then gently poached. For lobster, allow 8 minutes for every 450 g (1 lb); for crab, 15 minutes for every 450 g (1 lb). Both can be bought precooked and the crab is often completely prepared and sold as dressed crab. Prawns can be bought raw (often frozen) when they are a grey / blue colour. They can also be purchased cooked (also often frozen), when they will be the bright pinky red that you associate with cooked shellfish. Prawns are sold shell on or shell off (peeled), but it is an easy job to remove the head, tail and legs.

Shellfish & safety

It is vital that all shellfish is fresh, otherwise serious food poisoning can occur. Make sure that you buy it either live, frozen or just cooked. Fresh mussels should be closed and unbroken. If they are a little open you can check if they are still alive by tapping them, if they are alive and still safe to eat they will close, if they don't they are dead and should be thrown away. Before cooking, you need to use a sharp knife to scrape the shells and remove the barnacles and hairy thread called the beard.

To shell prawns

Pull off the prawn's head with your thumb positioned under the legs (1). Then, unwrap the shell from around the tail and the legs should come off with the shell on the back (2). Then, just gently pull off the final tailpiece (3).

Cooking Methods for Fish

Like meat, fish is made up of muscle fibres that vary in length. The fibres have very little connective tissue and this breaks down very easily during cooking. It is easy to overcook fish, resulting in it falling apart and becoming dry. Some fish do not have a very strong flavour and so simplicity and quick cooking is recommended.

How do you tell if fish is cooked?

Raw fish is translucent and glassy looking. As it cooks it quickly becomes opaque. When it is hot through to the centre, it will be cooked. The perfectly cooked piece of fish is just turning from translucent to opaque. When learning to cook anything, it is a case of trial and error. Why not cook an extra piece of fish so you can cut it and pierce with a skewer to see whether it is cooked? To test the fish, insert a metal skewer into the thickest part and leave for 15 seconds. Then, remove and test on the back of your hand. Do this quickly – if the skewer is very hot (too hot to hold against your hand) the fish is cooked. Salmon is often served a little underdone, slightly glassy in the centre but still hot. Tuna can be served rare when it has a butter-soft texture; if tuna is allowed to cook fully through it will be dry and fibrous. Some people prefer it that way, as they do with a well-done steak. It is often all about personal taste.

Ways of cooking fish

All fish should be seasoned with salt and pepper prior to cooking, and served as soon as it is cooked, unless it is to be flaked into a salad and served cold, for example, a fresh tuna salad.

Steaming

Steaming is a great way to cook fish, as many of the vitamins – and indeed aspects of the flavour – are water-soluble; by steaming you won't lose anything to the liquid. Try it in a steamer, or wrapped in leaves such as spinach or banana leaves.

Poaching

Poaching means cooking gently in barely bubbling liquid. This could be water flavoured with peppercorns, bay leaves and a little vinegar or milk, as in a fish pie (see p. 62), where the liquid is used for the sauce.

Cooking Methods for Fish

Griddling

This is much the same as pan frying but uses oil not butter. The griddle pan must be almost smoking hot. Use firm steaks or fillets, as the fish is liable to break up. These tips also apply if you are barbecuing your fish.

Pan frying

This method of cooking is great for fillets or fish steaks. Melt a little butter or oil in a pan and allow the pan to heat up so the butter foams. Place the fish in the pan. Make sure the fish browns on one side before you turn it, and then brown the other side. The fish should be cooked by now but use the skewer test on thick pieces of fish.

Roasting

This method is superb with larger portions of fish such as tuna or cod loin. Preheat the oven to 200°C / 400°F / gas mark 6. Place fish portions of the same size (so it all cooks at the same rate) in a roasting tin; do not allow them to touch. Flavour with olive oil, garlic and perhaps some lemon and roast uncovered for between 8–15 minutes. Use the skewer test to check the fish is cooked before serving.

Grilling

Grilling is suitable for delicate pieces of fish that would break up if moved about too much, for example, fillets of sole. Preheat the grill and place the fillets onto an oiled baking sheet (this could be sprinkled with herbs or crumbs). Cook without turning as the metal baking sheet conducts the heat to cook from beneath. Exact cooking times are difficult as fillets can be different sizes. A more accurate way is to keep monitoring and cook until the flesh changes from translucent to opaque and the fish is extremely hot.

Deep or shallow frying

For this method the fish is coated in egg and breadcrumbs (or batter) to protect it from the fierce heat. Allow the oil to get really hot; test it by adding a crust of bread – if the oil is hot enough it should brown gently in about 15–20 seconds. Remove the bread and fry the fish in small batches. Drain on kitchen paper and sprinkle with salt to remove excess oil and to season. Remember, fish cooks very quickly so keep a close eye on it.

Cheese

If you've got eggs and cheese in the fridge, then you'll always be able to rustle up something quick and tasty.

Cheese is always made from milk, although taste and texture will vary tremendously, depending on the milk used and how it's been made. Choosing types of cheese is down to personal taste and depends upon what you are selecting the cheese for: whether for a particular recipe or for a cheese board.

There are several ways to categorise cheese; here are some types and their uses:

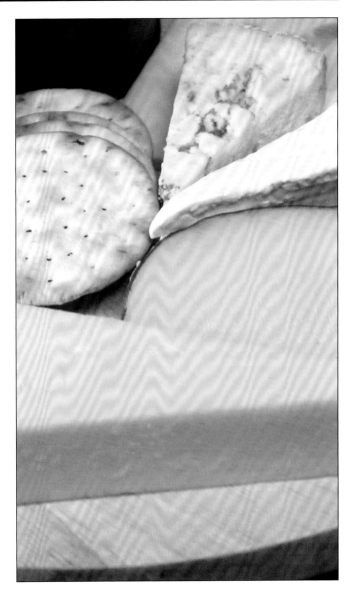

- **Fresh unripened cheese** – Uncured and unripened, such as fromage blanc and fresh ricotta. These are not aged and must be used at once. They often have a sharp flavour and are wonderful served with fruit. These also include cream cheese for cheesecakes, good mozzarella for salads and the cheaper kinds for melting on pizzas.
- **Soft cheeses** – Brie, Camembert and Dolcelatte. Used for cheese boards, spreading on bread and in cooking.
- **Semi hard** – Edam, Gouda, Stilton and some Cheddars. Used for cheese boards and in cooking.
- **Hard** – Cheddar, Emmental, Gruyère. Used for cheese boards and in cooking.
- **Very hard** – Parmesan. Used for cooking and shavings to garnish.

Cheese

Storing cheese

Ideally, cheese should be wrapped in paper or cheesecloth and stored in a cool cellar. For most, this is just not possible so it is best to store it in the fridge in a plastic bag or cling film. Unwrapped cheese will dry out and crack. Mass produced cheese will always be the same and somewhat characterless. A good cheese shop should only sell cheeses that are ready to eat, therefore at their peak.

Cheese boards

One good cheese can be served at the end of a meal rather than lots of smaller pieces, but for a more varied choice go for one hard cheese, one soft cheese and perhaps a fresh cheese, such as goats' cheese. Cheese should be served at cool room temperature, so allow it to have a few hours out of the fridge before serving. Accompany with fruit, such as grapes, figs, apples and celery, and chutneys can also provide a tangy contrast to the cheese. Keep it simple and choose just one or two of the above to go with the cheese and don't forget the crackers.

Cooking with cheese

Some cheeses melt better than others, and it is this that determines which cheese to use in a particular recipe. Cheese becomes tough and stringy if overheated and this should be avoided. A good melting cheese is high in fat and not too dry.

Hot tip

Buy a lump of fresh Parmesan without too much rind. You can grate it when you need it or take off shavings with a potato peeler to garnish salads. It keeps well in a large piece, wrapped up in cling film and kept in the fridge. At all costs, avoid packet Parmesan cheese, which smells and tastes like bad feet!

Eggs

Eggs are so useful and versatile, from setting custards to lifting cakes and soufflés. They should be kept in the fridge and away from strong smells, as they are porous and things such as onions can taint them.

Hot tip

To tell if eggs are fresh, place an egg in a bowl of cold water. If it floats it is not fresh. This is because the egg has a small air sack in it, and the older the egg, the larger the air sack becomes. You may also spin the egg. If it spins on the spot it is fresh. Again this is due to the air sack becoming larger and sending the egg off centre.

Separating eggs

To separate the yolk from the white, crack the egg on the edge of a bowl and then open it with the pointed end uppermost (do this over the bowl). The yolk will be in the bottom half and most of the white will drop into the bowl. Then, carefully pour the yolk from half to half until all the white has gone. If you do break the yolk you can lift out any yolk bits from the white using the shell.

Cooking eggs

- To fry an egg: heat a little butter in a pan until barely hot; break the egg into the pan and leave to cook gently.

- To poach an egg: bring a small pan of water to the boil. Add a tablespoon of vinegar (this helps to set the protein in the egg). Take an egg straight from the fridge and break it into a cup. Swirl the water in the pan with a spoon. Drop the egg into the middle and immediately turn the pan down to simmering. You may follow it with another egg as the first egg swirls round the pan. It really works! When the eggs are cooked, remove with a slotted spoon and allow to drain briefly on kitchen paper.

- For a perfect omelette for one: break two eggs into a bowl and season with salt and pepper. Beat with a fork until well mixed. Heat a thumb-sized knob of butter in an omelette pan and allow it to foam. Tip in the egg mixture and let it cover the bottom of the pan. As it cooks draw the edges into the middle with a fork. Keep going with this until the eggs are almost set, but a little creamy in the centre. Remove the pan from the heat and tip the pan so that the omelette slides over to one side of the pan. Add your prepared filling to one side and, using a fork, fold the omelette in half. Have your plate ready and tip the omelette onto it.

- Scrambled egg is similar to making an omelette, but you stir the egg in the saucepan with a lot more vigour and do not let the bottom set. You may also add a little milk to the eggs.

- To cook boiled eggs: place the eggs in a pan of cold water and bring to the boil, simmering for 10 minutes for hard-boiled eggs and 4 minutes in already boiling water for a soldier-dipping yolk. Alternatively, add your eggs to a pan of boiling water, turn down the heat and simmer for 12 minutes. Place the harad boiled eggs in cold water to cool rapidly before peeling.

When cooking meals every day and shopping perhaps only every few days or once a week, it pays to have a well-stocked store cupboard or larder. You may buy meat or vegetables with no real idea of what they will become. However, if the store cupboard has everything it should have, then making any recipe or idea from a book, the Internet or your imagination can easily be achieved. You don't have to go out and buy all of these at once; just buy them as you need them and replace them when necessary, and soon you'll find your store cupboard is brimming with ideas.

Basics
Use olive oil and sunflower oil for cooking. Plain flour is useful for batters and gravy, as well as for cake making if you add raising agents such as baking soda. For thickening sauces, keep cornflour. This should be mixed into a paste with a little cold water before adding to your sauce.

Baking
It doesn't take many ingredients to knock up a quick sponge cake or a few biscuits and if you keep a number of stock ingredients in supply you'll be able to make a number of sweet treats whenever you fancy. Self-raising flour has the raising agent already in the flour and is great for making cakes. Baking powder, bicarbonate of soda, cream of tartar and cocoa powder are also useful for baking and making cakes. A number of sugars and sweetening agents are useful. Have a supply of the following and you'll be able to complete most recipes:

- icing sugar
- soft brown sugar
- demerara sugar
- caster sugar
- golden syrup
- clear honey

Baking and dessert recipes often call for vanilla, either vanilla essence or pods. Stay clear of the bottles labelled 'flavouring', which have a poor taste in comparison.

Buy some good quality cooking chocolate (look for cocoa solids of 70 percent). If you can't find decent cooking chocolate, buy good-quality eating chocolate with a high cocoa solids percentage.

Nuts, such as pine nuts, hazelnuts, walnuts and almonds are all great for baking and can also be used to jazz up salads. You'll find nuts sold either whole, chopped, flaked or ground; stock up on what you use most frequently or, if you have a food processor, buy them whole and prepare them yourself as required.

Dressings, sauces, marinades and gravies

Don't overlook the ingredients needed to make your accompanying sauces. If you use poor-quality ingredients in the condiments then your perfectly-cooked dish could be ruined.

For simple dressings, sauces, marinades and gravies keep the following in stock:

- Mustards – these are a great way to inject flavour into a dressing or plain white sauce to serve with ham or a gammon steak. Mustards don't like to be boiled, so add them at the end of the cooking and whisk in. Try wholegrain mustard, Dijon mustard or English mustard and appreciate the differences in each.
- Vinegar – red wine vinegar, white wine vinegar and balsamic vinegar are all good for salad dressings, as is extra virgin olive oil.
- Stock cubes – have a supply of beef, chicken, fish, lamb and vegetable cubes.
- Wine – decent red and white wine can be used for marinades, gravies and stews – as a guide you'll have a far tastier sauce if you use a wine you'd drink rather than a bottle of plonk.
- Table sauces – for stir fries and marinating, keep a supply of soy sauce, Asian fish sauce (nam pla), oyster sauce, plum sauce, Worcestershire sauce, tabasco sauce, tomato purée and tomato sauce.
- For quick pasta dishes, keep such things as tinned tomatoes, tapenade (black olive paste), olives, sun-dried tomatoes (dried or in oil), salted capers, tinned anchovies and pesto.

Carbs

There are plenty of dried options that should have a permanent home in your cupboard.

Dried pasta is really useful, and rice is a brilliant store cupboard stand-by. Also, try couscous – pour on enough boiling stock or water to just cover the couscous and cover with a plate. After a few minutes, stir with a fork. Add chopped herbs and lemon juice for a delicious taste.

Tinned pulses are a real winner. You can make a super cassoulet or tuna salad with tinned beans. Try chickpeas, borlotti, cannellini, butter, red kidney, or haricot beans.

Similarly, lentils are a great alternative to potatoes. Cooked with stock and finished with herbs, they taste fantastic.

Cooking dried pasta

Add the pasta to a pan of boiling, salted water. Use about 85 g (3 oz) pasta per person for a main course portion. Stir as the water comes back up to the boil and cook without a lid for the recommended time. The pasta should be al denté, just cooked, and if you cut the pasta in half there should be no starch visible. Drain to finish.

Cooking rice

Allow 50 g (2 oz) uncooked rice per person. Begin by washing the rice in cold water, using a sieve. Then, place the rice into a pan of boiling, salted water. Stir as the water returns to the boil and turn down to a simmer. Leave uncovered. Cook for 8–10 minutes (brown rice will take a bit longer – always check the timings on the packet for recommended cooking times) and test by eating a bit. It should feel tender and if you cut a grain in half it should have no white starch visible in the middle. Strain immediately and rinse with boiling water. Stir through any fresh herbs, cooked peas or chopped peppers for colour. For lemon-scented rice, cook as above and stir through the zest of two lemons and some freshly chopped coriander.

Herbs and spices

Clever experimentation with herbs and spices can lead to some great flavours. It may take time to develop a well-stocked collection, but drop an item into the trolley each week and let your imagination run wild.

The bare essential to your supplies should be salt and pepper. Rock sea salt and whole black peppercorns in particular are necessary for your salt and pepper mills.

Spices are useful for both sweet and savoury dishes. Try ground all-spice, ground cinnamon, ground coriander, ground cumin, ground ginger, garam masala, cardamom pods, cayenne, chilli powder, chilli flakes, peppercorns, paprika and turmeric. Remember to buy spices in small quantities as they lose their flavour if kept for too long. Dried herbs are also good items. They are particularly good in stews. Start with oregano, basil, mixed herbs and thyme.

Although dried herbs win on convenience, fresh herbs still have more flavour. Try fresh home-grown herbs.

In the fridge

Stock the fridge with staples, such as butter, milk, eggs, and cheese. Obviously, these cannot be purchased too far in advance, as they need to be used while still fresh.

Sundries

There are always other ingredients that will be needed:
• Fresh white bread for making crumbs.
• Citrus fruits – oranges, lemons and limes. Add them to a dressing or use them to flavour fish.
• Dried mushrooms provide masses of flavour for stews, rice and pasta dishes and make great stock.

Now you should have all you need. Some of the ingredients that have been featured are particularly suited to certain methods of cooking, but don't be limited by this. Experiment and enjoy!

Health and Safety

To avoid food poisoning it's important to make sure that the food you make for yourself and others is safe to eat. There are a few basic rules to help you make sure of this.

Buying
Only buy fresh food from sources that you trust.

Washing
Wash all food if it is to be eaten raw, even if the food is to be peeled, such as carrots and potatoes.

Your fridge
This should stay roughly at 4°C. It is important not to overfill it as this cuts down on circulation of the cool air. Refrigerate all meat, fish, chicken, dairy products and eggs. Keep dairy products at the top of the fridge and always cover raw meat and store it on the bottom shelf of the fridge where it can't touch or drip onto other foods. Try to rotate the food in your fridge and cupboards, so the oldest stuff is eaten first. Never put warm or hot food in the fridge as this will warm up the temperature inside. Wait until it reaches room temperature before refrigerating.

Raw meat
Raw meat contains harmful bacteria that can spread very easily to anything it touches, including other foods, worktops, chopping boards, hands and knives. It's especially important to keep raw meat away from ready-to-eat foods, such as salad, fruit and bread. As these foods won't be cooked before you eat them, the bacteria that gets onto these foods won't be killed. To help stop bacteria from spreading, remember these things:

- Don't let raw meat touch other foods.

- Never prepare ready-to-eat food using a chopping board or knife that you have used to prepare raw meat, unless they have been washed thoroughly first.

- Always wash hands, knives, boards and anything else in contact with raw meat or fish with cold water first to wash off the meat juices, then with hot soapy water and scrub well. Allow items to air dry before putting away and ensure that boards stand upright with air able to circulate around them.

- Change cloths and tea towels at least once a day.

- Use an anti-bacterial spray on kitchen surfaces before and after each cooking session.

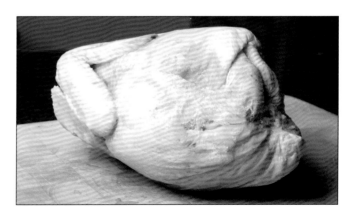

Health and Safety

Cooking

Always make sure you preheat the oven before placing food inside. Cook food thoroughly to kill any bacteria that may be present. Remember that pregnant women cannot eat raw or unpasturised eggs, so watch out in particular for mayonnaise dishes and make sure all eggs are thoroughly cooked. The old and very young may have lower immune systems and therefore also need well-cooked eggs.

Reheating food

If you need to reheat food, make sure that it is hot in the centre, and when keeping food warm, make sure it is thoroughly hot first, then maintain a good holding temperature that will keep it really hot, not just lukewarm.

Freezing & thawing

When freezing food, label and clearly mark with the date. Never refreeze thawed food without cooking it first. Thaw food overnight in the fridge, on a plate or in a plastic container in case of drips. Allow enough time for food to completely thaw; in the case of a Christmas turkey this could take a couple of days.

Cooling

When cooling food for storage, try to cool it as fast as possible, so bacteria doesn't have time to grow. Never cover with a lid while cooling, as this slows things down. Never cover with cling film either as this acts just like a

lid and provides warm, humid conditions, perfect for bacteria. Never leave food out overnight to cool; try to get it in the fridge within an hour of cooking.

If anything smells or looks bad, don't eat it. Food which actually looks 'off' is probably well on its way to deteriorating.

Food Presentation

People eat with their eyes first and if food looks fresh and inviting then you are off to a good start. Always make time to present the food on nice plates or in larger dishes; there is nothing worse than that 'chuck it on the plate' version of presentation.

Serving at the table can be rather fraught, and there is also the risk of the food getting cold by the time everyone is served. So it is often preferable to present individual servings, which can be arranged in the kitchen and brought straight to the table. This kind of service must be done on hot plates or your food will quickly go cold.

Whether it is rustic and homely food, or if you are having a stab at a more up-market presentation, the rules are the same. Here are some simple guidelines to ensure well-presented, stylish and delicious-looking food.

- Keep it hot; always serve food on hot plates. Don't plan complicated presentations or the food will get cold.

- Keep it simple and fresh looking. Remember, less is more when playing with food. Don't try to be too clever; keep the presentation clean and uncluttered.

- The right crockery is important if you want to impress with your presentation. Large white plates are in vogue at present and allow the food to speak for itself. The space also allows the cook to create more interest in the food. Whatever you choose, however, ensure that the plates are in keeping with the food. Use rustic bowls to serve spaghetti and other homely types of food and elegant white china for more stylish cuisine.

- Keep the garnish relevant and edible. For example, a sprig of fresh watercress complements lamb nicely. The texture, taste and colour all do something for the lamb and you can happily eat it; in contrast, a bunch of rosemary, even though it might provide the colour and relevant fragrance, is unpleasant to eat. When adding garnish to salads or trifles, placing olives or cherries in a pattern may sound like a good idea but it can look childish. In general, avoid symmetry when arranging food and remember odd numbers work better than even, especially smaller numbers.

Food Presentation

- Centre height: when serving any food that can be nicely piled up, such as meringues or profiteroles, or even pieces of meat in a casserole, try to arrange them with centre height rather than flat across the plate. This makes it look interesting and draws the eye to the food – it also helps keep things warm. When garnishing food with centre height, place the garnish to one side rather than in the middle or on the top.

- The right amount: ensure the plates of food look like a generous portion. If you don't have enough of something it just looks stingy to use a tiny bit. On the other hand, don't fill the plate to capacity just because you want to use something up.

- As a handy guide for when you're eating out, or even if you want to impress at home, opposite is a diagram of a formal table setting so you know exactly what to use and for what. As a general rule, use the outer cutlery first and work in towards the plate.

1. Napkin
2. Fish / starter fork
3. Dinner fork
4. Salad fork
5. Service plate
6. Soup bowl
7. Dinner knife
8. Fish / starter knife
9. Soup spoon
10. Bread plate
11. Butter knife
12. Dessert spoon and fork
13. Water glass
14. White wine glass
15. Red wine glass

Using the Recipes

As well as a drink suggestion, each recipe has a difficulty indicator. This is a rating out of five, one being the easiest. Here's a breakdown of what to expect from each rating:

1. Easy. In fact, you may already have made a recipe like this before.

2. Moments of confusion, but you'll soon get into the swing of things.

3. A few complicated bits, but it's likely to just be issues of timing rather than anything too fiddly.

4. Your skills might be stretched by dishes at this level but keep your cool and you'll be fine.

5. Tackle these dishes when you're more confident. The results will always be worth the effort but it's wise to give yourself plenty of time when cooking these recipes. They tend to use several skills and techniques.

Don't shy away from the more difficult dishes; if you never attempt the harder ones you'll never improve. Invite friends round and experiment on them if you don't want to force your efforts onto your partner or guests just yet.

The other information you'll find for each recipe includes preparation and cooking times. Don't be put off by these either. Often, a long preparation time will mean you can prepare it in advance and cook later. Similarly, a long cooking time generally means that you'll be able to leave it in the oven and get on with something else. Always read the recipe through before you begin, then you'll know exactly where the tricky parts are and you'll be far less likely to miss out vital ingredients.

Most of the recipes serve four people, but you can easily divide or multiply the quantities to correspond with your number of guests.

Home-made Burger

Home-made Burger

Fantastic to barbecue and so easy to make. They freeze well and are so much better than ones you buy.

You will need:
- 675 g (1½ lb) lean best steak mince
- 1 medium onion, peeled and grated
- 3 tbsp finely chopped parsley and chives
- 1 tbsp Worcestershire sauce
- salt and freshly ground black pepper
- a pinch of cayenne pepper (optional) or, a dash of tomato sauce (optional)

Preparation time: 15 minutes
Cooking time: 8 minutes
Serves: 4–6
Level of difficulty: 2
Drink suggestion: robust red wine or beer

1. Place all of the ingredients into a large bowl, and, with a clean hand, mix until completely combined.

2. Drape a piece of cling film over a plate. Divide the mince into six lots, then place a large pastry cutter* on a plate on top of the cling film. Press the mixture down into the cutter and smooth flat with your fingers or a spoon.

3. Remove the cutter, then use the cling film to move the burger to another plate.

4. Repeat with the remaining mixture and chill the burgers until you are ready to cook.

5. Thoroughly preheat the grill or barbecue, cook each side for 3–5 minutes until the burger is cooked to your preference. When you first put them onto the barbecue don't try to move them for at least 2 minutes; they will easily be turned with a fish slice after that time if the barbecue is hot enough.

***Note:** *Use a large pastry cutter to shape the burgers and they never fall apart. If you don't have a cutter, just shape them by hand. The burgers can be frozen once shaped. Just defrost overnight in the fridge on a plate or tray.*

Beef Chilli

Beef Chilli

Without the chilli and kidney beans this recipe can be used as a meat sauce base for bolognese, lasagne and cottage pie. Serve it with rice, tortillas, tacos, as a pancake filling or with jacket potatoes.

You will need:
- 450 g (1 lb) lean minced beef
- 1 large onion, finely chopped
- 1 stick of celery, finely chopped
- 2 garlic cloves, peeled and crushed
- ½ teaspoon chilli flakes (or more, if you like it hotter)
- 800 g (1 lb, 12 oz) 2 tins chopped tomatoes
- 300 ml (½ pint) beef stock (1 beef stock cube and water)
- 400 g (14 oz) 1 tin red kidney beans, drained
- salt and freshly ground black pepper

Preparation time: 30 minutes
Cooking time: up to 2 hours in the oven
Serves: 4
Level of difficulty: 2
Drink suggestion: light red wine

1. Heat a large heavy frying pan until it is quite hot but not smoking – you shouldn't need oil as there should be enough fat in the meat. Add the minced beef and spread it out over the base of the pan. Allow it to brown well, turning frequently and breaking it up as it browns. Tip the mince into a sieve while you cook the sauce.

2. Lower the heat and add a tablespoon of fat to the pan (you can use the fat draining off the mince for this). Add the onion and celery, cover and gently sweat the ingredients. When the onions and celery begin to soften, add the garlic and dried chillies and cook for a few more minutes.

3. Add the tomatoes, stock and browned mince and bring to the boil. Add the kidney beans and turn the heat down very low to simmer for 1–1½ hours, stirring now and again to prevent it catching, or see the hot tip below for oven cooking.

4. At the end of reducing the sauce, it should be slightly syrupy and the meat tender. Season with salt and freshly ground black pepper and accompany with rice (see p. 30).

Hot tip: Once you have added the kidney beans you can transfer the chilli to an ovenproof casserole dish with a lid and cook in the oven for two hours on 150°C / 300°F / gas mark 2. Long, slow cooking will give you a really tender and rich finish. Once the meat is tender, you can simmer in the oven without a lid to evaporate some of the liquid and concentrate the flavour.

Roast Chicken with all the Trimmings

Roast Chicken with all the Trimmings

A roast dinner never fails to impress and although it may seem daunting, it really isn't that hard to master.

For the stuffing:
- 2 tbsp sunflower oil
- 1 red onion, finely chopped
- 1 celery stick, finely chopped
- 4 garlic cloves, peeled and crushed
- 1 tsp thyme and rosemary, chopped
- 225 g (8 oz) pork sausage meat
- 1 apple, grated with skin
- 85 g (3 oz) fresh white breadcrumbs (place bread into a food processor to make crumbs)
- salt and freshly ground black pepper

For the chicken and chipolatas:
- 1.35 kg (3 lb) free-range chicken without giblets
- ½ an apple
- sprigs of thyme and rosemary
- salt and freshly ground black pepper
- 8 chipolata sausages
- 8 rashers of streaky bacon

For the gravy:
- ½ litre (1 pint) water
- 2 tsp plain flour
- 1 chicken stock cube

For the potatoes and vegetables:
- 8 medium-sized potatoes (maris piper, King Edward or desirée)
- sunflower oil or dripping, this could be the fat leftover from a previous roast or you can buy it as a solid block in the refrigerated section of your supermarket
- 450 g (1 lb) vegetables. Choose two or three vegetables of your choice, for example, mangetout, sugar snap peas, broccoli, courgettes or carrots. Use around 100 g (4 oz) veg per person (see p. 12–14 for cooking times and methods) or use the recipe for quick roasted vegetables (see p. 80).

Preparation time: 15–30 minutes
Cooking time: 2 hours
Serves: 4
Level of difficulty: 5
Drink suggestion: almost any wine

Roast Chicken with all the Trimmings

To make the stuffing

1. Heat the oil in a small saucepan and add the onion, celery and garlic. Cook with a lid for 10 minutes on a low heat until soft. Remove and place onto a plate to cool.

2. When the onion is cold, mix together all of the remaining ingredients for the stuffing and season well. You can fry a bit in a pan with a little oil to check the seasoning.

Preparing the chicken

1. Using your finger, lift the skin at the neck end and slowly release the skin from the breast. Work at it and you should create enough space for most of the stuffing.

Once the skin is released all over the breast, push the stuffing up and over the flesh. You want about 1 cm (½ in.) of stuffing over the whole area. Once you start, you can move your hand over the outside of the skin to evenly distribute the stuffing. The remaining stuffing (or all of it, if you don't fancy stuffing the breast) can be formed into golf ball-sized balls.

2. Place the apple and herbs inside the cavity of the bird. Season with salt and freshly ground black pepper. Place into a roasting tin, cover loosely with foil and put it in the fridge until you want to cook it.

3. To prepare the bacon, use the side of a knife to stretch out the rashers. Cut in half widthways and roll each half into a tight roll, pinning them together with a cocktail stick. Place the bacon rolls into a small roasting tin with the chipolatas and stuffing balls. These can also be prepared in advance.

Roast Chicken with all the Trimmings

To cook the chicken

1. Preheat the oven to 200°C / 400°F / gas mark 6. The chicken will need an hour and a half in the oven. (See p. 19 for other cooking times if your bird is smaller or larger.) Place the chicken in the middle of the oven. After 30 minutes remove the foil.

2. After one hour, place the chipolatas, bacon rolls and stuffing balls on the top shelf to cook.

3. After an hour and 15 minutes, test the chicken. Cut down between the breast and the leg. Let the leg fall open and use a knife to cut down to the thighbone. There should be no blood or pinkness.

4. If it is not yet cooked, return to the oven in another roasting tin, the other is needed to make the gravy. If it is cooked, remove the chicken and place onto a plate or a clean tin. Cover with foil and allow to rest while you make the gravy. It will stay hot.

To carve

Use a knife to remove the legs and cut in half at the joint. Using a sharp carving knife, cut slices from the breasts. The stuffing may become dislodged, but you can serve this alongside the chicken. Carve onto a large platter and cover with foil until you are ready to serve. Each person should get one piece of leg or thigh and some breast and stuffing. Alternatively, once you have removed the legs you can use kitchen scissors to completely remove the two breasts from the carcass. Then, cut each breast in half again. You should have four pieces of leg and four pieces of breast which can then be served between your guests.

Roast Chicken with all the Trimmings

To make real gravy

1. Add half of the water to the roasting tin, scrape up the sediment with a wooden spoon and then pour all of the juices from the tin into a small glass bowl, retain the roasting tin. Spoon off as much of the fat from the top of the juices as is possible, placing one tablespoon back in the roasting tin. The rest of the fat can be discarded but keep the juices which will be used later.

2. Place the tin on the hob over a very low heat and allow it to spit a bit; this is the water content evaporating, leaving only fat.

3. Add two teaspoons of plain flour to the fat and stir well with a wooden spoon. Continue to stir and scrape, allow the mixture to brown gently, but don't allow it to smoke.

4. Once it is a good biscuit brown add the chicken juices from your glass bowl, the rest of the water and the stock cube. Turn up the heat and allow it to boil and reduce down to a thin, syrupy consistency, adding any extra juices from the resting chicken. This will take a good 5 minutes giving you time to carve the chicken. If you feel you need to you can sieve the gravy. Add more water if it looks too thick.

Roast Chicken with all the Trimmings

To make roast potatoes

1. Preheat the oven to 200°C / 400°F / gas mark 6.

2. Use potatoes, such as maris piper, King Edward or desirée, for best results. Wash, peel and cut them into large even-sized pieces. Place into a pan of cold, salted water and bring to the boil with the lid on. Keeping the pieces large prevents them from absorbing too much water. You will cut them into roasting potato sizes later on.

3. Turn down to simmer for 5–10 minutes until barely tender. They should not be fully cooked. This is called par boiling. Place 5 tablespoons of sunflower oil or dripping into a roasting tin and place in the oven while it heats up.

4. Drain the potatoes (you can reserve the water for making the gravy) and allow to steam for 5 minutes. Return to the pan and shake to roughen the edges. This will give a crispier finish.

5. Check the fat in the oven. Once it's really hot, add the potatoes and cut each in half with a cutlery knife. This roughens the edges further. Shake the roasting tin gently and turn the potatoes with a fish slice to coat them in the oil.

6. Place into the oven for 45 minutes to an hour, turning twice with the fish slice during cooking. When done they will have a rough crusty edge and be deep golden brown. Season with salt and pepper before serving.

Timings for roast dinner

This assumes you have prepared the chicken and all of your vegetables beforehand, which should only take 15–30 minutes.

11:00   Preheat the oven.

11:15   Chicken in the oven.

11:40   Par-boil the potatoes. Heat the oil for the roast potatoes.

12:00   Drain and roast potatoes. Move the chicken down to the bottom shelf of the oven to make room for the roast potatoes. Turn the potatoes at least twice during their cooking time.

12:15   Put the bacon rolls, chipolatas and stuffing balls in the oven. You can put them around the chicken if you are short of oven space.

12:40   Check the chicken – if it is not cooked, return it to the oven in a different roasting tin while you make the gravy.

12:45   Gravy making and cooking of other vegetables (depending on cooking time of chosen vegetables). If your potatoes and trimmings are nice and brown, turn the oven off, but keep the door closed to keep everything hot.

12.50   Carve the chicken.

12:55   Remove all of the trimmings from the oven and serve.

1.00   Dining.

Warm Chicken Salad

Warm Chicken Salad

Serve this chicken salad as a lunch or a light supper – it's perfect for a summer's day when stoking up the barbecue seems too much effort.

You will need:
- 4 chicken breasts, trimmed of fat and skin
- 2 tbsp plain flour
- salt and freshly ground black pepper
- 2 tbsp of sunflower oil

For the salad
- 4 handfuls of mixed small salad leaves, such as rocket, watercress, lollo rosso, little gem; a prepared mixed bag is also a good option
- 3 tbsp olive oil
- 1½ tbsp balsamic vinegar
- salt and freshly ground black pepper
- 12 cherry tomatoes
- ½ cucumber, cut into large cubes

Preparation time: 20 minutes
Cooking time: 15 minutes
Serves: 4
Level of difficulty: 1
Drink suggestion: light red or white wine

1. Cut the chicken breast into large pieces, about eight pieces from each breast.

2. Mix together the flour, salt and freshly ground black pepper. Roll the chicken in the flour mix and remove to a plate. Put the chicken pieces into a sieve to remove any excess flour.

3. Heat the oil in a large, heavy frying pan until hot, but not smoking. Roll the chicken once again in the flour and shake off the excess using the sieve.

4. Fry the chicken in batches, about twelve pieces at a time. Cook the chicken until it is golden brown and firm to the touch. It should take about 4 minutes. You may need to add a little more oil for the second batch. Place the chicken on kitchen paper once cooked while you assemble the salad.

5. Wash and dry the salad and mix the dressing by whisking the olive oil and balsamic vinegar together. Season with salt and freshly ground black pepper.

6. Place the salad in a large bowl with the cherry tomatoes, cucumber and dressing. Mix carefully and serve onto four plates. Put the chicken pieces on top of the salad and serve at once.

Toad in the Hole

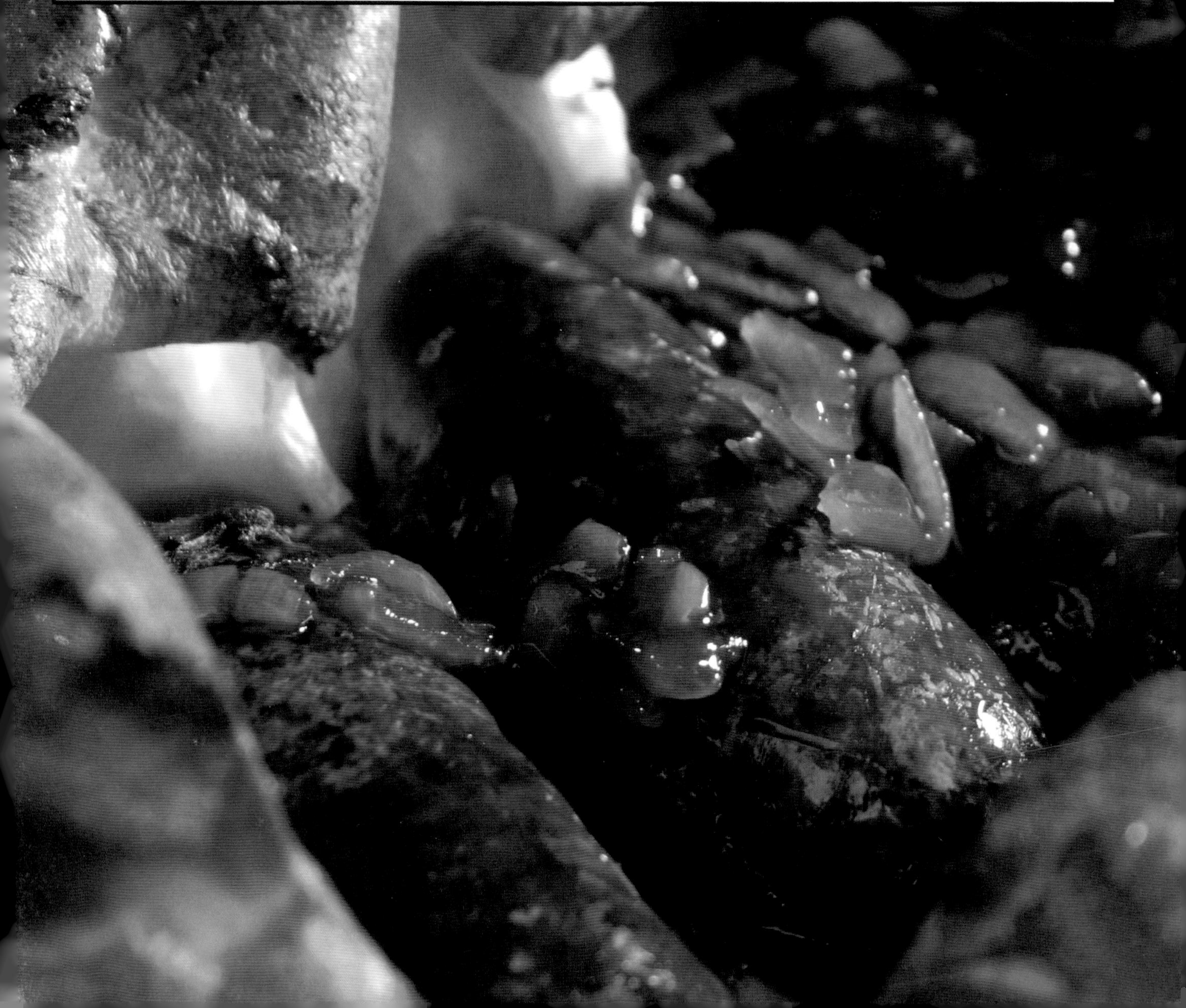

Toad in the Hole

For a more fancy toad you can serve individual ones cooked in little, flat ovenproof dishes. Have two sausages per dish and cook for about 15–20 minutes. They can be served in their dish as well. The batter recipe can also be used to make Yorkshire puddings for a roast dinner.

You will need:
- 100 g (4 oz) plain flour
- a good pinch of salt
- freshly ground black pepper
- 3 large eggs, beaten
- 300 ml (½ pint) full fat milk and water mixed, or 300 ml (½ pint) semi-skimmed milk
- 8 large good-quality sausages
- 4 tbsp beef dripping, vegetable or sunflower oil

Preparation time: 40 minutes
Cooking time: 45 minutes
Serves: 4
Level of difficulty: 3
Drink suggestion: Côtes-du-Rhone

1. Sift the flour, salt and pepper into a large bowl. Make a hole in the centre.

2. Put the beaten eggs into the hole and, working in a small circular motion, begin to incorporate the flour. When half of the flour is mixed in, begin to add a little of the milk and water.

3. All of the flour should be mixed in by the time half of the milk is added. Beat the batter to make it smooth and lump free, then add the remaining liquid.

4. Sieve the batter if it contains lumps and chill for 20–30 minutes.

5. Meanwhile, brown the sausages by frying them in a pan with a little of the oil or dripping. Preheat the oven to 220°C / 425°F / gas mark 7.

6. Heat the remaining dripping or oil in a shallow but large roasting tin, either in the oven while it preheats or over a direct heat. When almost smoking, place the sausages in at intervals and pour over the batter. Place in the top part of the oven and cook for at least 40 minutes, or until the batter is risen, brown and crisp. Do not open the oven for the first 20–25 minutes as the batter will not rise properly. Glass-fronted ovens are great if you want to be able to peek at your food. Cut and serve with vegetables, such as broccoli or green beans and onion gravy. If you like your toad with mash then see p. 63.

Toad in the Hole

For the gravy you will need:

- 1 tbsp sunflower oil
- 1 medium onion, finely sliced
- 1 tsp plain flour
- 2 tbsp red wine / madeira / port
- 400 g (14 oz) tinned French onion soup or beef consommé
- salt and pepper

Preparation time: 5 minutes
Cooking time: 15 minutes
Level of difficulty: 1

1. Heat the oil in a small pan and add the sliced onion. Cook gently for 10 minutes with the lid on to soften.

2. Turn up the heat and brown the onion. When brown, add the flour, stir in and continue to cook.

3. When both the onion and flour are brown, add the red wine, madeira or port. Gently stir in.

4. Add the French onion soup or beef consommé. Bring to the boil and cook for about 5 minutes, or until thickened and slightly syrupy.

5. Taste and season with salt and pepper. Serve over your toad in the hole.

Spicy Sausage and Chickpea Soup

Spicy Sausage and Chickpea Soup

This is a real winter warming soup, good and chunky with a spicy kick to it.

You will need:

- 1 large pinch saffron strands (optional)
- 2 tbsp olive oil
- 225 g (8 oz) mini chorizo sausage or similar, cut into small cubes
- ½ tsp dried chilli flakes
- 2 garlic cloves, peeled and finely chopped
- 400 g (14 oz) tinned chopped tomatoes
- a pinch of sugar
- 400 g (14 oz) tinned chickpeas, drained
- 285 g (10 oz) new potatoes, quartered lengthways
- 1 bay leaf
- 1 litre (1¾ pints) vegetable stock
- salt and pepper
- 4 tbsp flat leaf parsley, freshly chopped (save a few leaves to garnish)
- chilli oil (to serve)

Preparation time: 15 minutes
Cooking time: 45 minutes
Serves: 4
Level of difficulty: 3
Drink suggestion: Italian or Spanish red wine

1. Soak the saffron (if using) in a little warm water and set aside for 10 minutes. Meanwhile, heat the oil in a large pan, add the sausage and cook for 2–3 minutes until golden brown. Drain and set aside.

2. Add the chilli flakes and garlic to the pan. Cook for 1–2 minutes. Stir in the tomatoes, sugar, chickpeas, potatoes, bay leaf, stock, saffron with its liquid and the sausage.

3. Bring to the boil, reduce the heat and simmer for 30 minutes with a lid on, stirring occasionally until the potatoes are cooked through and the mixture thickens slightly. Season with salt and pepper

4. Stir in most of the fresh parsley and spoon into individual soup bowls. Drizzle with a little chilli oil, sprinkle with the remaining parsley and serve with plenty of crusty bread.

Hot tip: *By cooking this without a lid you can reduce the cooking liquid and make it into a thick stew instead of a soup.*

Lamb Cutlets with Spicy Couscous

Lamb Cutlets with Spicy Couscous

If you always struggle with cooking rice give couscous a try. A north African staple, couscous doesn't really need much cooking and is ready in 5 minutes. With quick cooked lamb cutlets this dish is real fast food.

You will need:

- 225 g (8 oz) couscous
- 300 ml (½ pint) tomato juice (leftover juice can be frozen in ice cube trays for future use)
- salt and freshly ground black pepper
- 25 g (1 oz) butter
- 1 tsp ground cumin
- ½ tsp ground coriander
- 1 green pepper, finely chopped
- ¼ tsp dried chilli flakes (you can always add more to taste, but start small)
- 4 tbsp chopped fresh herbs, such as parsley, coriander, mint
- 12 trimmed small lamb cutlets
- 1 tbsp sunflower oil
- sprigs of mint to garnish

Preparation time: 15 minutes
Cooking time: 10 minutes
Serves: 4
Level of difficulty: 2
Drink suggestion: French medium red wine

1. Place the couscous into a large bowl. Bring the tomato juice to the boil, season with salt and freshly ground black pepper and pour it over the couscous. Add some extra boiling water to just cover the couscous, cover the bowl with cling film and leave for 5 minutes.

2. Melt the butter in a large pan and slowly fry the spices, add the chopped green pepper and as much of the dried chillies as you want, then cook for another minute.

3. Fluff up the couscous with a fork and add it to the spices pan, stir gently, taste and season again. Then, add the fresh herbs and keep warm.

4. Heat a griddle pan, frying pan or grill and season the lamb cutlets. Add oil to the pan and allow it to get quite hot, but not smoking. Place the cutlets into the pan and cook each side for 3 minutes, until they are cooked but still pink in the centre.

5. Pile the couscous onto four plates, arrange the cutlets on top and add a sprig of mint to garnish.

Home-made Pizza

Home-made Pizza

The time and effort needed to make your own pizza dough may seem excessive, but the results are worth it. This recipe makes a light, crispy base, in keeping with the traditional pizzas you get in Italy.

You will need:
- 450 g (1 lb) strong plain flour
- 1 heaped tsp salt
- 1 tsp fresh rosemary, finely chopped (optional)
- ½ tsp cracked black pepper
- ½ tsp dried yeast (1 sachet)
- ½ tsp of sugar
- 300 ml (½ pint) lukewarm water
- olive oil for brushing
- extra flour for kneading and shaping
- 350 g (12 oz) good-quality thick fresh tomato sauce (1 jar)
- 200 g (7 oz) grated mozzarella cheese

Preparation time: 15 minutes, plus dough rising time of up to an hour
Cooking time: 10 minutes
Serves: 4
Level of difficulty: 3
Drink suggestion: Chianti

1. Line a bowl with olive oil and sift the flour and salt into it. Mix in the rosemary (if using), pepper, yeast and sugar. Add nearly all of the water and mix to a soft dough with a knife. You may not need all of the water.

2. Knead for 5 minutes on a floured surface. Place into a clean bowl and cover with cling film. Leave to rise in a warm place for 40 minutes or longer until double in size.

3. While the dough is rising, prepare the pizza toppings (see p. 57 for ingredients). Tear or cut the ham, use a vegetable peeler to make Parmesan shavings, quarter the olives and so on.

4. Preheat the oven to 220°C / 425°F / gas mark 7.

5. Divide the dough into four pieces, shape into rounds and, with a rolling pin, roll each one as thinly as you can into a circle. Sprinkle flour over your baking trays to prevent sticking and transfer the dough bases. Leave them to rest just as long as it takes you to roll out the other bases, during which time they will shrink a little. Roll over each base again, while still on the tray, so that they are about 25 cm (10 in.) across.

see p. 57 for ingredients

Home-made Pizza

For your topping choose from:

- 4 slices thick cut parma or prosciutto ham, torn into pieces (streaky bacon would work too)
- 25 g (1 oz) Parmesan cheese for shavings
- a handful of black olives
- a few capers
- a few anchovies
- pepperoni slices
- sliced peppers
- 12 sun-dried tomatoes, finely chopped
- rocket or basil to garnish

6. To assemble the pizzas, take a large spoonful of the tomato sauce and spread thinly over the base, leaving a 2 cm margin around the edge.

7. Sprinkle over the mozzarella cheese and arrange the other topping ingredients over the pizza. Make sure there is not too much topping or the base will not cook.

8. Bake in the hot oven for about 10 minutes or until the base is crisp and brown underneath.

9. Serve garnished with Parmesan shavings and some rocket.

Hot tip: *If you don't have room in the oven to cook all of the pizzas at once, they will hold, once made, for up to 30 minutes.*

Lemon, Garlic and Rosemary Roast Cod

Lemon, Garlic and Rosemary Roast Cod

Most fish has a delicate flavour, so it's best to cook it simply – even the familiar cod can be turned into something special with only a few ingredients and the omission of batter!

You will need:
- 8 tbsp olive oil
- 8 cloves of garlic, with the skin still on
- 4 sprigs of rosemary
- 2 lemons, each cut into 6 wedges
- 4 thick pieces of cod fillet, about 170 g (6 oz) each with the skin left on
- 1 tbsp plain flour, seasoned with salt and pepper

Preparation time: 15 minutes
Cooking time: 15 minutes
Serves: 4
Level of difficulty: 2
Drink suggestion: dry French white wine

1. Preheat the oven to 200°C / 400°F / gas mark 6.

2. Place the oil, garlic, rosemary and all but four of the lemon wedges in a roasting tin, squeezing the wedges as you put them in. Put in the oven for 10 minutes to allow the oil to infuse. This can be done well in advance if you have time. Reheat for 5 minutes when you are ready to cook.

3. Check the fish for bones, leave the skin on and pat dry with kitchen paper. Dip the fish into the seasoned flour on the skin side only, shaking off the excess.

4. Remove the lemon, rosemary and garlic while you brown the fish, but do not discard.

5. Put the roasting tin directly on a hob. When the oil is hot, carefully place in the seasoned fish, skin side down. When the skin side is golden brown, turn the fillets, replace the lemon, rosemary and garlic and cook in the oven for 10–15 minutes, or until the flesh is opaque and the flakes of fish begin to give when pressed. Serve with mashed potatoes (see p. 63) and some roast tomatoes.

Ultimate Fish Pie

Ultimate Fish Pie

By going to the fishmonger you can buy a fillet or a small chunk of any fish. If you say you want it for fish pie the fishmonger will help you make it up to 900 g (2 lb). You can use any combination of fish for your pie – try getting haddock, salmon and a bit of smoked cod. Once you are a dab hand you can try adding scallops or prawns.

You will need:
- 425 ml (¾ pint) milk
- ½ onion, sliced
- 6 black peppercorns
- 1 bay leaf
- 2 tbsp parsley – chop the leaves but leave the stalks whole
- 900 g (2 lb) fish filets with skin on
- 25 g (1 oz) butter
- 25 g (1 oz) flour
- salt and freshly ground black pepper
- 3 tbsp double cream (optional)
- 4 hard-boiled eggs (see p. 27)
- 1.13 kg (2 ½ lb) mashed potato, see p. 63

Preparation time and cooking time: about 1 hour
Serves: 4–6
Level of difficulty: 4
Drink suggestion: dry white wine

To poach the fish
1. Preheat the oven to 180°C / 350°F / gas mark 4.

2. Heat the milk in a roasting tin with the onion, peppercorns and bay leaf. If you have parsley stalks bash them with a rolling pin and add to the milk.

3. Lay the fish fillets in the roasting tin, skin side up, cover with foil and cook in the oven for 15–20 minutes. (When you are using scallops and shellfish, add these for the last 5 minutes of the cooking time.)

4. When the fish is just cooked (see pp. 23–24), remove the skin from the fillets, checking for bones. Do this by tucking the prongs of a fork under the skin, gently twisting and rolling the skin around it (see picture below). With a fish slice, remove the fish from the milk to a plate, remove the peppercorns and bay leaf, and sieve the milk to use for the sauce.

Ultimate Fish Pie

To make the white sauce

1. Heat the butter in a pan and add the flour, stir with a wooden spoon for 2 minutes. This is called a roux.

3. Bring to the boil, stir for 2 minutes and taste. Season with salt and freshly ground black pepper.

4. Remove from the heat and add the double cream (if using) and chopped parsley.

2. Now, slowly add some of the milk (kept from poaching the fish) stirring all of the time. The sauce will become thick and you should beat it steadily to remove any lumps. Slowly add the rest of the milk while continuing to stir.

Ultimate Fish Pie

To make the mashed potato
You will need:

- 900 g (2 lb) maris piper potatoes, washed, peeled and cut into even-sized chunks
- 2 tsp salt
- 300 ml (½ pint) creamy milk
- 50 g (2 oz) unsalted butter
- salt and freshly ground black pepper

Preparation time: 5 minutes
Cooking time: 20 minutes
Level of difficulty: 1
Serves: 4

1. Place the prepared potatoes in a large pan of cold water. Add the salt and bring to the boil. Cover with a lid and simmer until the potatoes are tender (about 15 minutes – test with a cutlery knife, it should sink into the potato when it's cooked).

2. Drain the potatoes in a colander and place back into the pan. Pour most of the milk into the pan and heat gently with the butter. Once steaming, mash with a potato masher and then season well with salt and freshly ground black pepper. Take care not to over stir the potato as it can go gluey. Add more milk if it is too firm. Delicious!

To assemble the pie

1. Place the fish into a large shallow ovenproof dish with the quartered hard-boiled eggs and pour the sauce evenly over the top. Stir if necessary but do this gently.

2. Spread or pipe (see p. 8) the potato on top. Return it to the oven to heat through (see reheating information below). If all of the ingredients are already hot it can just be flashed under the grill to brown the potato.

Hot tip: *This pie freezes well so you can make two and freeze one. Allow to defrost in the fridge overnight and reheat for 30–60 minutes at 190°C / 375°F / gas mark 5, depending on the size of the pie. Always check that the pie is thoroughly heated all the way through.*

Chilli and Parsley Pesto with Barbecued Tuna

Chilli and Parsley Pesto with Barbecued Tuna

Pesto is traditionally made with basil, but this recipe substitutes parsley, a herb that complements the flavours of the tuna steak perfectly; the added chillies give a great kick too. You will need a blender for this recipe, but if the weather isn't up to a barbecue, then cook the tuna in a griddle or frying pan.

You will need:
- 4 thick tuna steaks, about 170 g (6 oz)
- 1 tbsp olive oil (for pan-frying and griddling)
- a large bunch of flat leaf parsley, stalks removed
- 2 green chillies
- ½ clove of garlic, bashed and peeled
- 1 tbsp pine nuts or almonds
- 7 tbsp olive oil
- 2 tbsp grated Parmesan cheese (optional)
- salt and freshly ground black pepper

Preparation time: 20 minutes
Cooking time: 5 minutes
Serves: 4
Level of difficulty: 2
Drink suggestion: Sauvignon Blanc

To make the pesto
1. Wash and roughly chop the parsley. Remove the stalk from the chillies, slice in half lengthways and remove the seeds if you don't want the pesto to be extra hot. Roughly chop the flesh of the chilli.

2. Place the parsley and chillies into a blender with the garlic. Blend for 2 minutes, then add the nuts and oil. You may have to turn the machine off to poke the mixture down with a spoon a couple of times as it does tend to stick. When it looks combined, add the cheese and season with salt and freshly ground black pepper. Store in the fridge in a sealed container such as a jam jar. The pesto will stay green for at least two weeks.

Hot tip: *If you want to make the pesto more of a sauce, just add some water when making it and it will emulsify like mayonnaise, giving you a bright green smooth sauce.*

To cook the tuna
1. Preheat the barbecue or grill.

2. Brush the tuna steaks with a little olive oil and season with salt and freshly ground black pepper. Place on the hottest part of the barbecue and leave for at least 3 minutes.

3. Use a fish slice or pallet knife to gently turn the steaks. They should not stick if the barbecue is really hot. Cook for another 3 minutes and transfer to serving plates and accompany with the pesto. Serve with chunky chips (p. 76).

Quick Mushroom Soup

Quick Mushroom Soup

A simple soup, full of flavour and a far cry from the 'cream of' varieties stacked high in the supermarket.

You will need:

- 25 g (1 oz) butter
- 1 small onion, finely chopped
- 1 small garlic clove, peeled and chopped
- 450 g (1 lb) mushrooms, (preferably flat caps), chopped
- 1 slice of bread, crusts removed
- 1 litre (1¾ pints) chicken or vegetable stock
- salt and freshly ground black pepper
- a pinch of nutmeg
- parsley stalks, bashed and tied with kitchen string
- 2 tbsp fresh chopped parsley (to garnish)
- single cream (optional)

Preparation time: 10 minutes
Cooking time: 30 minutes
Serves: 4
Level of difficulty: 1
Drink suggestion: light, dry white wine

1. Melt the butter in a large heavy-based saucepan. Add the onion, sweat (cook gently without colouring the onions) for 10 minutes.

2. Add the garlic and the mushrooms and cook slowly for 10 minutes, stirring while they soften. Crumble in the bread and stir again to combine.

3. Add the stock, seasoning, nutmeg and tied parsley stalks (this way you get the flavour without the annoying bits of stalk) and bring to the boil. Simmer for 10 minutes.

4. Remove the parsley stalks and string, liquidise and sieve the soup if you want. This is not necessary if you want a rustic finish.

5. When you are ready to serve, re-heat the soup, garnish with parsley and finish with a little cream.

A note about cooking with cream: *Single cream normally contains about 18 percent fat and must not be boiled. When using it for soups or sauces it should be added at the end of cooking and carefully reheated. Double cream has about 48 percent fat and is stable enough to be boiled. It is perfect for sauces that are made by reducing down the flavours to make them more intense. If you want something less rich in flavour, try crème fraîche, which is also high in fat and can be boiled. If using one that is low in fat (such as half fat crème fraîche), treat it like single cream.*

Spinach and Blue Cheese Pasta

Spinach and Blue Cheese Pasta

A classic combination of flavours that's even easier than spag bol to cook!

You will need:

- 1 tsp salt
- 340 g (12 oz) dried pasta, tagliatelle, tubes or twists (allow 85 g (3 oz) of dried pasta per person)
- 4 tbsp olive oil
- 2 small onions, finely chopped
- 2 garlic cloves, peeled and crushed
- 170 g (6 oz) frozen spinach or 340 g (12 oz) fresh spinach
- 4 tbsp crème fraîche
- 170 g (6 oz) blue cheese, such as Dolcelatte or Gorgonzola, cut into cubes
- salt and freshly ground black pepper

Preparation time: 10 minutes
Cooking time: 15 minutes
Serves: 4
Level of difficulty: 1
Drink suggestion: Italian dry white or light Italian red

1. Bring a large pan of water to the boil. Add a teaspoon of salt and cook the pasta according to the instructions on the packet. It should be al denté, which means soft, but retaining a slight bite to the teeth (see the note opposite).

2. While the pasta is cooking, heat the oil in a shallow pan and cook the onion and garlic gently for a few minutes. Remove to a plate.

3. Add the spinach to the pan and cook until it thaws out or wilts. If using fresh spinach, you will need to drain and squeeze it before continuing.

4. Return the onion and garlic to the pan and add the crème fraîche and blue cheese.

5. Add the cooked, drained pasta to the pan. Mix well, taste and season with salt and freshly ground black pepper. Serve immediately.

A note on cooking pasta: *To check whether pasta is cooked, you can simply eat a bit. It should feel cooked but not chewy. Alternatively, you can cut a piece in half and it won't have a white, starchy middle once it's cooked.*

Sun-dried and Cherry Tomato Risotto

Sun-dried and Cherry Tomato Risotto

Risotto is an often overlooked Italian dish, but it's a great alternative to pasta and this dish makes a satisfying meat-free meal.

You will need:

- 1.70 litres (3 pints) vegetable stock
- 85 g (3 oz) sun-dried tomatoes, chopped
- 50 g (2 oz) butter
- 1 tbsp olive oil
- 2 small red onions, chopped
- 2 small garlic cloves, peeled and crushed
- 400 g (14 oz) arborio (risotto) rice
- 1 tbsp bought pesto sauce (optional)
- 100 g (4 oz) oyster or field mushrooms, sliced
- salt and freshly ground black pepper
- 225 g (8 oz) cherry tomatoes, washed
- 50 g (2 oz) Parmesan cheese
- chopped fresh flat-leaf parsley, to garnish

Preparation time: 20 minutes
Cooking time: 40 minutes
Serves: 4
Level of difficulty: 3
Drink suggestion: Australian Shiraz or Italian red wine

1. In a large saucepan, heat the vegetable stock with the sun-dried tomatoes over a medium heat.

2. Heat the butter and oil in another large pan. Add the onions and garlic and cook, stirring occasionally for 5 minutes, or until soft.

3. Add the rice and cook, stirring, for one minute. Add the pesto sauce (if using) and cook for a further 3–4 minutes. Begin to add the stock, a ladleful at a time, bring to a simmer, stirring occasionally, until the liquid has been absorbed. Continue slowly adding the stock, allowing it to be absorbed in between.

4. Stir in the mushrooms and season with salt and pepper. Simmer until all of the liquid has been absorbed and the rice is tender and creamy. You may need to add a little more stock. It should take about 30 minutes for the rice to cook. Add the tomatoes to heat through in the last 5 minutes of cooking.

5. Using a vegetable peeler, shave curls of Parmesan cheese over the risotto, sprinkle with parsley and serve.

Vegetable Curry with Lemon-scented Rice

Vegetable Curry with Lemon-scented Rice

A satisfying curry that's great as a main course or side dish.

You will need:
- 1 tbsp sunflower oil
- 1 red onion, sliced
- 1 carrot, peeled and finely diced
- 2 garlic cloves, peeled and crushed
- 225 g (8 oz) potatoes, peeled and diced
- 1 tbsp medium curry paste (adjust to taste)
- ½ tsp ground coriander
- 1 tsp peeled and grated fresh ginger
- 400 g (14 oz) tinned chopped tomatoes (1 tin)
- 400 g (14 oz) tinned chickpeas, drained (1 tin)
- 150 ml (¼ pint) vegetable stock
- salt and freshly ground black pepper
- a handful fresh coriander, chopped
- 50 g (2 oz) uncooked basmati rice per person
- zest of two lemons

Preparation time: 30 minutes
Cooking time: 30 minutes
Serves: 2 as a main dish or 4 as a side dish
Level of difficulty: 2
Drink suggestion: Indian Beer

1. Heat the oil in a large saucepan. Add the onion, carrot and garlic and cook on a low heat for 10 minutes with a lid on. Add the potatoes, curry paste, ground coriander and ginger and cook, stirring, for a further 5 minutes.

2. Add the tomatoes, chickpeas and vegetable stock, bring to the boil and cook uncovered for 15 minutes, stirring every few minutes to make sure it doesn't stick.

3. Check the potatoes are tender and season with salt and freshly ground black pepper. If you think the curry is too dry, add a little stock or water. If too wet, boil rapidly to evaporate any excess liquid. Add the fresh coriander and serve with naan bread and / or lemon-scented rice (see p. 30).

Red Onion Omelette

Red Onion Omelette

This recipe is delicious as a breakfast, starter or light meal and it's fantastic hot or cold. Once cooked it can be kept in the fridge for up to a day. You will need a 23 cm (9 in.) non-stick omelette or frying pan; if making this for two people use a 14 cm (6 in.) pan and half the ingredients.

You will need:
- 1 tbsp olive oil
- 25 g (1 oz) butter
- 3 large red onions, peeled, halved and sliced
- 6 eggs
- salt and freshly ground black pepper
- a good pinch of paprika
- 50 g (2 oz) Parmesan cheese, grated

Preparation time: 15 minutes
Cooking time: 30 minutes
Serves: 4
Level of difficulty: 1
Drink suggestion: Côtes-du-Rhone

1. Heat the oil and butter on a medium heat in the non-stick frying pan.

2. Add the sliced onions, stir and cover with a plate or lid. Lower the heat and cook slowly until soft, stirring occasionally. This is called sweating and will take about 15 minutes.

3. Meanwhile, crack the eggs into a bowl and season with salt, pepper and paprika.

4. Add the Parmesan cheese and beat with a small whisk or fork until well mixed. Once the onions are soft, pour the egg mix onto the onions and turn the heat right down.

5. Cook very slowly for 15 minutes; the eggs should be set and the surface slightly runny.

6. Place the pan under a preheated hot grill for a few minutes to brown the top. It will feel firm when cooked.

7. Slide onto a plate and serve cut into wedges.

Chunky Chips

Chunky Chips

These chunky wedge chips are great as a snack on their own or to serve with any number of dishes, especially a home-made burger (p. 36).

You will need:
- 4 large potatoes (1 per person) cara, desirée or King Edward
- 4 tbsp olive oil (1 tbsp per potato)
- salt and pepper

Preparation time: 5 minutes
Cooking time: 25–35 minutes
Level of difficulty: 1
Serves: 4
Drink suggestion: light red wine or beer

1. Preheat the oven to 200°C / 400°F / gas mark 6. Wash the potatoes and cut each one into 6–8 wedges – leave the skins on.

2. Place the wedges into a plastic or glass bowl with an inch of water, cover with a plate and microwave for 5–10 minutes so that a knife just penetrates the potatoes. Carefully check after 7 minutes to see how they are doing.

3. Heat the olive oil in a roasting tin and add the potatoes, coat in the oil, adding the garlic and herbs, if using (see hot tip), and roast in the oven for 20–30 minutes, or until deep golden brown and crisp. Drain on kitchen paper and season with salt and pepper.

Hot tip: *Crushed garlic left in its papery skin and herbs (particularly rosemary and thyme), make tasty additions to these chips. Add the herbs and garlic as the potatoes go into the oven.*

Garlic Baked New Potatoes

Garlic Baked New Potatoes

This method of cooking in a bag is called 'en papillote'. Any quick cooked item can be done in this way. Try cooking a piece of fish instead of the potatoes – it will only take about 10 minutes. Fruit can also be cooked this way – try bananas and apricots wrapped in foil.

You will need:
- 750 g (1 lb, 10 oz) new potatoes, washed
- 4 garlic cloves
- 4 tsp olive oil
- salt and freshly ground black pepper
- 2 sprigs thyme, very finely chopped
- 2 springs rosemary

Preparation time: 5 minutes
Cooking time: 45 minutes to 1 hour
Serves: 4
Level of difficulty: 2
Drink suggestion: light red wine

1. Preheat the oven to 200°C / 400°F / gas mark 6. Cut two large heart shapes from greaseproof paper, each half of the heart should be at least as large as an A4 piece of paper, 21 cm (8 in.) x 30 cm (12 in.).

2. Divide the potatoes into two lots. Place a pile of potatoes and two unpeeled garlic cloves onto one side of each heart shape.

3. Drizzle each with half the oil, season with salt and freshly ground black pepper and add the thyme and rosemary.

4. Fold the heart in half and starting with the rounded top edge begin to make small folds to seal the edges of the paper. One fold should secure the previous fold. Finish with a twist at the point.

5. Place on a baking sheet (you may need two sheets if the parcels are too big) and bake for about 45 minutes to an hour. Test they are done by poking the potatoes through the paper with a skewer. The potatoes will brown beautifully through the paper, and you can serve straight from the paper.

Roasted Vegetables

Roasted Vegetables

Roasting is such an easy way to serve vegetables, a one-tray wonder which vegetarians and meat eaters alike will love.

You will need:
- 900 g (2 lb) total weight of vegetables for 4 people (choose from: firm, slow-cooked vegetables; carrots, celery, new potatoes, swede, turnip, leek, or baby onions. Softer quicker-cooked vegetables; aubergine, courgettes, celeriac, parsnip, Brussels sprouts, butternut squash or sweet potato)
- olive oil
- thyme and rosemary sprigs
- salt and freshly ground black pepper

Preparation time: 15 minutes
Cooking time: 1 hour
Level of difficulty: 1
Drink suggestion: light red wine

1. Preheat the oven to 200°C / 400°F / gas mark 6. Choose a combination of the listed vegetables, wash, peel and cut into large cubes, about the size of a small Brussels sprout.

2. Place the firm vegetables into a roasting tin with a few tablespoons of olive oil, herbs, salt and freshly ground black pepper. Stir well, then cover with foil and place on the top shelf of the oven.

3. After 20 minutes, add the prepared softer vegetables, stir carefully and return to the oven without the foil. Cook for another half an hour and stir carefully twice during the cooking time. Check the vegetables are tender and slightly caramelised.

4. Serve with any roast dinner or your favourite main course.

Hot tip: *Cubes of bacon are delicious cooked with vegetables. The addition of herbs, such as thyme and rosemary, will also give a wonderful aromatic flavour. Alternatively, add some honey towards the end of the cooking time and return to the oven for a really golden, mouth-watering finish.*

Easy Chocolate Mousse

Easy Chocolate Mousse

This recipe is a synch; it just involves being organised and then going for it. The crème fraîche in this recipe gives this mousse a more adult flavour, but you can use extra thick double cream if you prefer.

You will need:
- 140 g (5 oz) good quality dark chocolate, broken up into chunks
- 2 eggs
- 150 ml (¼ pint) crème fraîche

Preparation time: 20 minutes
Chilling time: 2 hours
Serves: 4–5
Level of difficulty: 2
Drink suggestion: Orange Muscat or Madeira

1. Melt the chocolate in a bowl placed over a saucepan of steaming water, known as a bain-marie. Alternatively, you can melt it in the microwave on the defrost setting. It will take about 5 minutes and you need to stop and stir every minute or so.

2. Remove the chocolate from the heat as the last few lumps melt. This prevents the chocolate becoming overheated, which can leave it looking dry and lumpy. Allow to cool.

3. Separate the eggs, putting the whites into a larger bowl, and the yolks into a cup.

4. When the chocolate is cool, but not setting, whisk the egg white until it just holds its shape – about 5 minutes with a hand-held non-electric whisk.

5. Still using your whisk, but with a stirring movement, rather than a whisking movement, add the yolks to the chocolate and stir briskly for 15 seconds. Add the crème fraîche and stir for a further 30 seconds.

6. Add half of the whisked egg white, stirring in. Then, add the remaining egg white and gently fold it in until mixed.

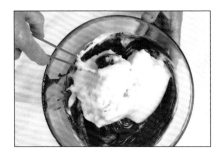

7. Place into glasses, ramekins or a medium-sized bowl and freeze for 30 minutes, or leave for a few hours in the fridge. Serve with posh biscuits.

Hot tip: *When melting chocolate, even a drop of water can make it stiff and lumpy, so be careful. If the chocolate has gone really lumpy you can add a knob of butter and blend it in. This should make it smooth again and allow you to continue with the recipe. The same applies if the chocolate is overheated and goes dry and grainy.*

Summer Fruit Pavlova

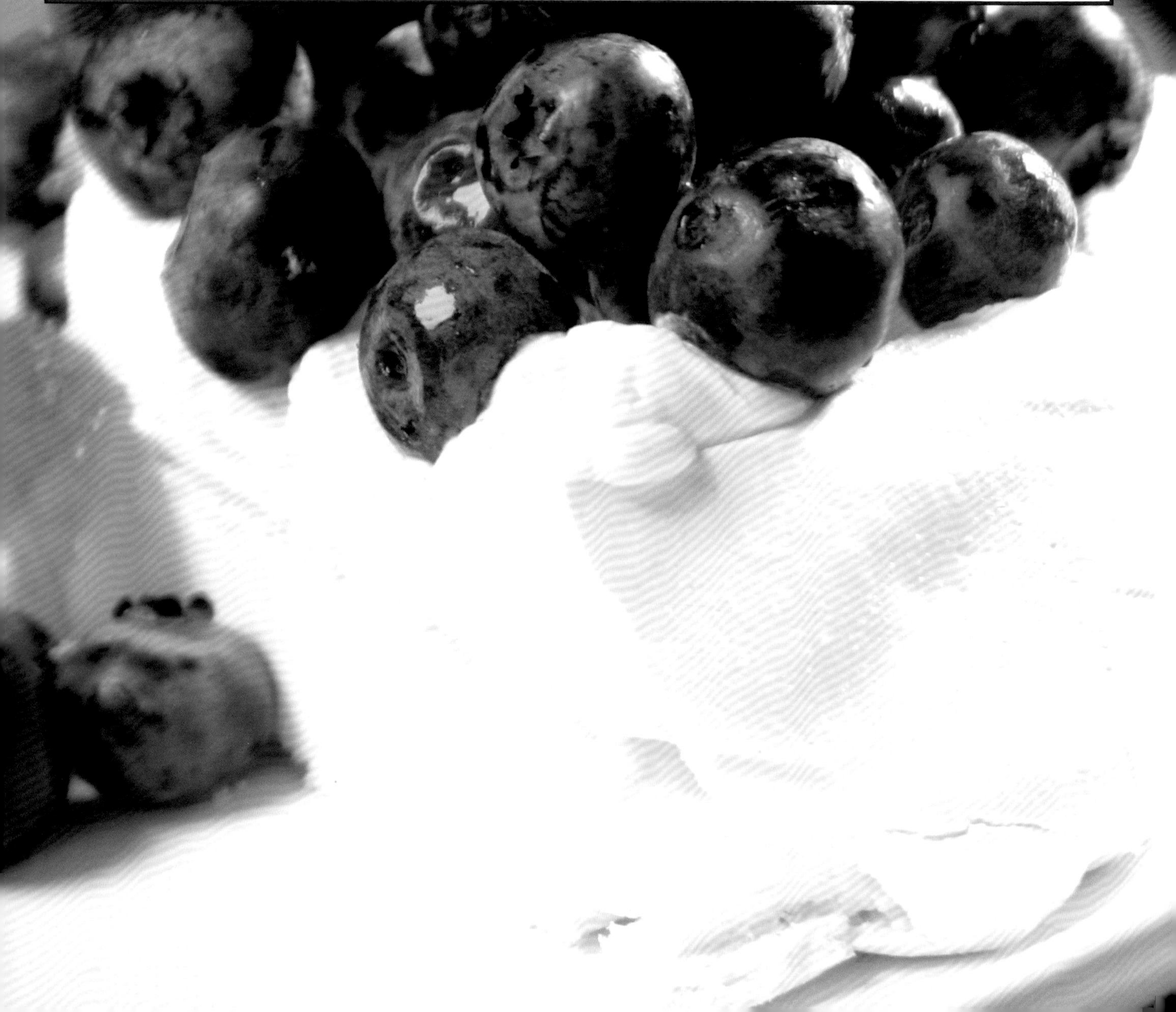

Summer Fruit Pavlova

A classic pudding that won't fail to impress. I've used blueberries in this example, but you could use any berry in season; raspberries are also particularly good.

You will need:
- 2 egg whites
- 100 g (4 oz) caster sugar
- ½ teaspoon cornflour
- ½ teaspoon white wine vinegar
- a few drops of vanilla essence
- 200 ml (⅓ pint) double cream
- 285 g (10 oz) raspberries or blueberries
- 4 sprigs fresh mint

Preparation time: **25 minutes**
Cooking time: **1 hour**
Serves: **4**
Level of difficulty: **2**
Drink suggestion: **muscatel or sweet sherry**

1. Preheat the oven to 130°C / 250°F / gas mark ½. Line a baking sheet with a piece of non-stick baking parchment.

2. Using an electric whisk, whisk the egg whites in a very clean bowl (any grease residue on the bowl will prevent the whites from stiffening). Whisk until the egg whites become fluffy and an opaque white and form soft peaks when you lift the beaters up.

3. Now, start to slowly add the caster sugar as you continue to whisk. The mix should begin to become stiff and very shiny. Continue to add the sugar in stages. By the end you should be able to stand a teaspoon up in the mixture.

4. Whisk in the vinegar, cornflour and vanilla.

5. Using a metal spoon or plastic spatula, transfer the mixture onto the baking sheet, spreading it out into a circle. Bake on the lowest shelf for about 45 minutes or until the meringue comes cleanly away from the paper. Remember that meringue is supposed to be soft and gooey in the middle. Allow to cool; it can be kept for a few days at this stage.

6. Whip the cream until it holds its shape. Spoon the cream into the middle of the meringue. Pile the blueberries on top of the cream, and garnish with a sprig of mint.

Note: *This recipe will make four small individual pavlovas. Just spoon four oval shapes onto the baking sheet and make a small dip in the centre of each. Cook at the same temperature for 45 minutes or until the meringue comes cleanly off the paper.*

Mixed Berry Frozen Yoghurt

Mixed Berry Frozen Yoghurt

Desserts don't come much easier than this! All you need is a working food processor and an index finger! Don't defrost the berries, you'll end up with a watery mush, use them straight from the freezer. The other thing about this recipe is that it's relatively diet-friendly, especially if you use half-fat Greek yoghurt.

You will need:
- 225 g (8 oz) mixed frozen summer fruits
- 450 g (1 lb) Greek yoghurt
- 3 tbsp cranberry and raspberry juice

Preparation time: 15 minutes
Serves: 4
Level of difficulty: 1
Drink suggestion: crème de cassis or raspberry liqueur

1. Place all of the ingredients into a food processor and whizz until everything is mixed. You may need to scrape the sides a few times to incorporate all of the berries.

2. Serve straight away in iced glasses, or you can keep in the freezer for up to two hours.

Mascarpone and White Chocolate Cheesecake with Berries

Mascarpone and White Chocolate Cheesecake with Berries

This gorgeous cheesecake will go down well at any dinner party!

You will need:
- 200 g (7 oz) digestive biscuits (about 12 biscuits)
- 50 g (2 oz) butter
- 170 g (6 oz) white chocolate, broken into pieces
- 250 g (9 oz) mascarpone cheese
- 1 tbsp orange or cherry liqueur
- 200 ml (7 fl.oz) crème fraîche (low fat is fine)
- 1 large punnet (about 200 g / 7 oz) of red berries, such as strawberries or raspberries. Use more or less according to taste
- mint to garnish

Preparation time: 20 minutes
Chilling time: 1 hour
Serves: 6
Level of difficulty: 2
Drink suggestion: sweet sparkling wine

1. Place the biscuits in a large food bag and crush with a rolling pin until they resemble breadcrumbs.

2. Melt the butter in a pan and add the crushed biscuits. Mix well and using a spoon, push tightly into the base of a shallow 20 cm (8 in.) loose-bottomed cake tin or flan ring. Chill in the fridge while you make the topping.

3. Put the chocolate and mascarpone into a glass bowl over a pan of barely simmering water. Stir to melt the chocolate and as the last few lumps are melting, remove from the heat and stir until smooth. Stir in the liqueur, then leave to cool slightly.

4. Stir the crème fraîche into the cooled chocolate mixture. Pour onto the biscuit base and leave to set in the fridge for about an hour.

5. Remove the cake tin or flan ring and serve piled with the berries. Garnish with mint.

Chocolate Sandwich Cake

Chocolate Sandwich Cake

Your reportoire wouldn't be complete without a good birthday cake!

You will need:
- oil (sunflower or vegetable) for greasing
- roll of parchment paper
- 225 g (8 oz) butter, kept at room temperature
- 225 g (8 oz) caster sugar
- 4 large free range eggs
- 200 g (7 oz) self-raising flour, sifted
- a large pinch of baking powder
- 25 g (1 oz) cocoa powder
- 150 ml (¼ pint) double cream, whipped
- fresh raspberries (optional)

Preparation time: 30 minutes
Cooking time: 30 minutes
Serves: 6–8
Level of difficulty: 3
Drink suggestion: sweet sherry or Madeira

1. Preheat the oven to 180°C / 375°F / gas mark 4. Prepare two 20 cm (8 in.) sandwich tins and line each one with parchment paper.

2. With an electric whisk, cream (beat) the butter with the sugar until the mixture is pale and fluffy. Beat the eggs and add them slowly to the creamed mixture, blending well between each addition.

3. Fold in the sifted flour, baking powder and cocoa. Add a tiny bit of water to bring the mixture to a dropping consistency.

4. Place the mixture into the prepared tins. Bake in the oven for 25 minutes, or until the mixture springs back when lightly pressed with a fingertip. Remove from the oven and allow to cool in the tins. Once cool, remove from the tins and discard the lining paper. Sandwich together with the cream or even crème fraîche. Dust with caster sugar. Alternatively, sandwich with a layer of cream, chocolate icing (see below) and fresh raspberries. Top with the chocolate icing as pictured.

To make a delicious chocolate icing

Place 150 ml (¼ pint) double cream in a small pan and bring to the boil. Break up or grate 100 g (4 oz) of good quality cooking chocolate into a bowl. When the cream comes to the boil (see notes on p. 67), remove from the heat and add the chocolate. Stir until melted and allow to cool slightly before spreading onto your cake. The icing will thicken as it cools, so put it on the cake before it sets! This quantity is enough to fill the cake as well as ice it, or you can make the extra into truffles or freeze it. Just warm it in the microwave on the defrost setting to melt it for your next cake.

Hot tip: *For a quicker cake, place all of the ingredients (except the cream) into a food processor and whizz until blended, then bake as usual. It may not be as light as the creamed cake, but not many will notice.*

Menu Suggestions

The beauty of being able to cook a number of different recipes is that you can combine them according to the occasion. Here are a few ideas about which dishes to put with which. These are only suggestions, and you can mix and match according to your preference. Equally, if you feel overawed by producing more than one dish for an event, you could concentrate on just producing one course using a recipe from this book, and buy in any other courses.

Dinner party:

Starter	Warm chicken salad
Main course	Lamb cutlets with spicy couscous or lemon, garlic and rosemary roast cod
Dessert	Easy chocolate mousse

What to do in advance:
- Chicken can be rolled in flour in advance and chilled
- Salad can be washed, but not dressed
- Dressing can be made
- The couscous can be cooked, ready to be reheated in the microwave with the herbs
- The chocolate mousse can be made a few hours before or even the day before

On the night
- Fry the chicken, dress the salad
- Fry the cutlets or roast the cod
- Cook accompanying potatoes / vegetables

Romantic dinner:

Starter	Spicy sausage and chickpea soup
Main course	Spinach and blue cheese pasta
Dessert	Mascarpone and white chocolate cheesecake with berries

What to do in advance
- Make the soup the day before and refrigerate
- The cheesecake can be made the day before

On the night
- Heat up the soup in a pan on the hob
- Cook the pasta dish

Menu Suggestions

Barbecue:

Buffet — Chilli and parsley pesto with barbecued tuna
Home-made beef burgers
Chunky chips
Leaf salad
Summer fruit pavlova
Mixed berry frozen yoghurt

What to do in advance
- Make the pesto
- Wash the salad
- Make the burgers
- Cook the meringue
- Make the frozen yoghurt, keep it in the freezer

On the night
- Cook the chips
- Cook the tuna and burgers on the barbecue
- Dress the salad
- Add the whipped cream and fruit to the pavlova

Roast dinner:

Starter — Quick mushroom soup
Main course — Roast chicken with all the trimmings
Roasted vegetables
Dessert — Easy chocolate mousse

What to do in advance
- Make the soup
- Make the chocolate mousse

On the night
- Reheat the soup
- Follow the timings for the roast dinner on page 45

Cooking for veggies:

Starter — Red onion omelette
Main course — Sun-dried and cherry tomato risotto
Dessert — Chocolate sandwich cake

What to do in advance
- Make the omelette (serve it as a cold dish)
- Prepare the risotto up to the point where you add the liquid
- Make the cake

On the night
- Complete the risotto dish

Healthy option:

Starter — Warm chicken salad
Main course — Ultimate fish pie
Dessert — Mixed berry frozen yoghurt

What to do in advance
- Roll the chicken in flour and chill
- Wash the salad
- Make the pie and freeze, then defrost the night before

On the night
- Fry the chicken and dress the salad
- Reheat the pie so it is heated all of the way through

Glossary of Terms

Al denté an Italian term describing food that is cooked so that it is firm to the bite (ie, not overcooked and floppy).

Bake blind the term for cooking pastry cases without a filling, just paper and baking weights to protect the pastry.

Bain-marie a French term for a roasting tin or saucepan half filled with water, into or over which you place your cooking dish. It protects food from fierce heat.

Basting to brush or spoon liquid fat or juices over foods being roasted, to encourage moistness during cooking.

Blanching cooking vegetables or fruits by plunging briefly into boiling water, to pre-cook, or retain colour.

Boil to heat liquid until it is a mass of quick moving bubbles.

Bouillon another name for stock.

Bouquet garni a small bundle of flavourings for soups and stews, usually thyme, rosemary, bay leaf.

Braising baking or stewing meat, poultry or vegetables in liquid in a covered pot.

Brown when cooking meat, this means cooking the outer edges of the meat (sealing) until it colours slightly.

Canapé a French term for bite-sized appetisers served with drinks.

Caramelise to allow the food cooking to turn to the colour and / or consistency of caramel.

Casserole refers to both the ovenproof dish and the method of slow cooking in the oven.

Creaming blending together butter and sugar, or a general mixing term to produce a smooth, cream coloured finish.

Croute a bread disc usually fried and used for carrying a topping.

Croutons small fried cubes of bread used for garnishing soups and salads.

Crudités sticks of raw vegetables for dipping into a thick sauce. Usually served as an appetiser.

Drizzle to drip or slowly pour a small amount of liquid over or around some food.

Emulsify to mix together two ingredients slowly and to form a smooth sauce such as mayonnaise.

En croute wrapped in pastry.

En Papillote food that is cooked in a bag of paper or foil.

Glossary of Terms

Flambé   French for flaming. Certain foods are sprinkled with alcohol, which is ignited before serving.

Fold   to use a large metal spoon to incorporate one mixture into another very gently.

Fry   to heat oil or butter in a pan and cook food allowing it to colour.

Griddle   to cook using a griddle pan, which is a heavy frying pan with ridges that scorch and pattern food.

Infuse   to mix ingredients with a liquid to impart their flavour, i.e tea is an infusion.

Julienne   term for vegetables cut finely into strips.

Marinate   to place food into a seasoned liquid (a marinade) to absorb flavour or in some cases to tenderise.

Mirin   low alcohol, sweet golden wine used in Japanese cooking.

Par-boil   to part cook potatoes or other vegetables in water.

Poaching   to cook by simmering gently in a liquid.

Purée   liquidised, sieved or finely mashed fruit or vegetables.

Prove   putting aside dough or yeast batter to rise before baking.

Reduce   to boil a sauce or liquid to intensify flavour and reduce quantity.

Refresh   to place cooked vegetables into cold water after boiling to stop cooking and keep their colour.

Relax or rest   to allow the pastry time in the fridge to settle, avoiding shrinkage. Joints of roasted meats are left to 'rest', which allows time for the juices to settle and makes for easier carving.

Roux   flour and butter cooked gently in a pan as a base for a sauce or gravy.

Sauté   to fry quickly in hot fat.

Seasoned flour   plain flour seasoned with salt and pepper.

Shredded   to finely cut into very thin ribbons. Used especially for vegetables.

Simmer   describes a liquid that is heated to a very gentle bubbling point.

Skillet   ridged frying pan, similar to a griddle pan.

Sweat   to cook vegetables very gently in a pan with butter, usually with a lid.

Whipped   hand whisked or whisked by machine to incorporate air.

Zest   the skin of any citrus fruit, thinly peeled and without the white pith.

Weights and Measures

It doesn't matter whether you work with metric or imperial measurements, just ensure you stick with one or the other throughout a recipe as the conversions are approximate. Also included are cup measurements that are favoured in the US.

Liquid

Imperial		Metric
1 tsp		5 ml
1 tbsp		15 ml
5 tbsp		75 ml
¼ pint	5 fl.oz	150 ml
½ pint	10 fl.oz	300 ml
¾ pint	15 fl.oz	425 ml
1 pint	20 fl.oz	570 ml
1¾ pint	35 fl.oz	1000 ml/1 litre

Oven Temperatures

115°C	240°F	gas mark ¼
130°C	250°F	gas mark ½
140°C	285°F	gas mark 1
150°C	300°F	gas mark 2
160°C	320°F	gas mark 3
180°C	350°F	gas mark 4
190°C	375°F	gas mark 5
200°C	400°F	gas mark 6
220°C	425°F	gas mark 7
235°C	450°F	gas mark 8

Weight

Imperial	US	Metric
¼ oz	1 tsp	7 g
½ oz	1 tbsp	15 g
1 oz	2 tsbp/ ⅛ cup	30 g
(a heaped tablespoon of flour weighs about an ounce)		
2 oz	¼ cup	50 g
3 oz	⅓ cup	85 g
4 oz/ ¼ lb	½ cup	100 g
5 oz	⅝ cup	140 g
6 oz	¾ cup	170 g
7 oz	⅞ cup	200 g
8 oz/ ½ lb	1 cup	225 g
9 oz	1⅛ cups	250 g
10 oz	1¼ cups	285 g
12 oz/ ¾ lb	1½ cups	340 g
14 oz	1¾ cups	400 g
16 oz/ 1lb	2 cups	450 g
1¼ lb	2½ cups	560 g
1½ lb	3 cups	675 g
2 lb	4 cups	900 g
3 lb	6 cups	1.35 kg
4 lb	8 cups	1.8 kg
5 lb	10 cups	2.3 kg
6 lb	12 cups	2.7 kg

Note: *Cup measurements are approximate and will vary according to the volume of your ingredients.*